Chores Without Wars

Other Books in the Developing Capable People Series

Positive Discipline A–Z: 1001 Solutions to Everyday Parenting Problems
Jane Nelsen, Lynn Lott, and H. Stephen Glenn

Positive Discipline in the Classroom: How to Effectively Use Class Meetings and Other Positive Discipline Strategies
Jane Nelsen, Lynn Lott, and H. Stephen Glenn

Positive Discipline for Single Parents: A Practical Guide to Raising Children Who Are Responsible, Respectful, and Resourceful
Jane Nelsen, Cheryl Erwin, and Carol Delzer

Raising Self-Reliant Children in a Self-Indulgent World: Seven Building Blocks for Developing Capable Young People
H. Stephen Glenn and Jane Nelsen

Positive Discipline for Parenting in Recovery: A Guide to Help Recovering Parents
Jane Nelsen, Riki Intner, and Lynn Lott

Positive Discipline for Teenagers: Resolving Conflict with Your Teenage Son or Daughter
Jane Nelsen and Lynn Lott

Positive Discipline: A Teacher's A–Z Guide
Jane Nelsen, Roslyn Duffy, Linda Escobar, Kate Ortolano, and Debbie Owen-Sohocki

Positive Discipline for Blended Families: Nurturing Harmony, Respect, and Unity in Your New Stepfamily
Jane Nelsen, Cheryl Erwin, and H. Stephen Glenn

Positive Discipline for Preschoolers
Jane Nelsen, Cheryl Erwin, and Roslyn Duffy

For a free newsletter from Capable People Associates, call (800) 456-7770.

Chores
Without Wars

Turning Dad and Kids from Reluctant Stick-in-the-Muds to Enthusiastic Team Players

Lynn Lott
Riki Intner

Prima Publishing

Library of Congress Cataloging-in-Publication Data

Lott, Lynn.
    Chores without wars : turning dad and kids from reluctant stick-in-the-muds to enthusiastic team players / Lynn Lott and Riki Intner.
        p.   cm.
    Includes bibliographical references and index.
    ISBN 0-7615-1252-7
    1. Parenting—United States. 2. Family—United States. 3. Home economics—United States. I. Intner, Riki. II. Lott, Lynn. Family that works together—. III. Title.
    HQ755.8.L676 1997   97-35409
    646.7'8—dc21   CIP

97 98 99 00 01 AA 10 9 8 7 6 5 4 3 2 1
Printed in the United States of America

How to Order
Single copies may be ordered from Prima Publishing, P.O. Box 1260BK, Rocklin, CA 95677; telephone (916) 632-4400. Quantity discounts are also available. On your letterhead, include information concerning the intended use of the books and the number of books you wish to purchase.

Visit us online at www.primapublishing.com

Contents

Foreword
by
Jane Nelsen

Why *Chores Without Wars?* Because Lynn and Riki's ideas are good for everyone in the family. It is not good for children to be pampered. They grow up thinking the world "owes them a living." It is not good for women to be "supermoms." By remaining slaves to their role stereotypes they are being disrespectful to themselves and their family members by doing too much for them, overprotecting them. And, supermoms usually harbor hidden or obvious resentments: Why doesn't my family appreciate me after all I do; why don't they do more for me when I do so much for them; why aren't they perfect when I try so hard to be perfect? Nor is it good for men to be slaves to their role stereotypes. They, too, are being disrespectful to themselves and their family. They miss the joy of equality and cooperation.

Instead of struggling with unrealistic stereotypes, families should try to incorporate a sense of *gemeinschaftsgefuehl* into their lives. *Gemeinschaftsgefuehl* is a German word coined by Alfred Adler. It is difficult to translate this term into English because it means so much, but "social interest" comes the closest. It means genuine concern for others, for the community, and for the environment. It means cooperation. It means taking action to contribute to others, the community, and the environment. *Gemeinschaftsgefuehl* (or social interest) is so important that Alfred Adler believed it to be a measure of mental health—the more social interest, the more mental health one has. Your family's success in performing chores without wars could be a measure of your family's social interest and mental health.

Chores Without Wars is a book that helps the whole family develop social interest, mutual respect, and so many other important life skills that will help your children be more successful in life. Much is being said today about the importance of good character, values, and emotional intelligence. All this can be learned through *Chores Without Wars*. This could be one of the most important parenting books you will ever read.

Acknowledgments

We'd like to thank all the families who shared problems and stories with us over the years so that our book could be practical and realistic. Mostly, we'd like to dedicate this book to our children and husbands with love and appreciation.

Introduction

Are you looking for help with messy rooms, dirty dishes, unmowed lawns, or reluctant helpers? Are your teenagers doing less while you are getting more aggravated? Do certain household members, untrained in the art of cooperation, think they are exempt from helping? Do family members help out only when threatened, nagged, bribed, and directed? *Chores Without Wars* offers suggestions to make things better for everyone in your home—whether there are two or ten of you.

In *Chores Without Wars* you will learn how to do the tasks that keep a household running smoothly in a cooperative, respectful, and enjoyable way. The suggestions in this book encourage self-respect and respect for others through the practice of shared decision making and cooperation. As you become more familiar with the methods in *Chores Without Wars,* you'll feel closer to other family members, be more willing to contribute, and replace conflict and chaos with feelings of belonging and camaraderie.

This is a book about families working together. We use the word "family" to define a group of people living together. No two families are alike. Look into any household and you will find some with two parents, children, and pets; others consist of unrelated adults sharing a house. There are families with one adult and one child, blended families with children moving back and forth between households, families with grandparents living in the home, and even families where children raise each other without much adult help.

When we talk about "working together," we are referring to those jobs and routines that benefit the entire family and are part of daily family living such as bedtime routine, caring for pets, doing dishes, cleaning the house, buying groceries, cooking dinner, putting gas and oil in the family car, mowing or watering the lawn, and doing the laundry.

It is easier to make changes if you have models. Therefore, we'd like to share stories of families who have benefited from the ideas suggested in *Chores Without Wars*. We would have been grateful for such examples when we changed from traditional moms and wives who thought we should do it all to women who learned to let go, share, teach, and include others. If you are ready to make a shift in your family, perhaps these vignettes will help you picture what you can achieve.

Accelerate Your Change Process With New Pictures

The Gregory family has two parents and two school-age children. In the morning Dad leaves before the rest of the family is awake, but first he walks the dog, then he feeds the cat on his way out. The children get up to their alarm clocks, clean their rooms, get ready for school, and make their own lunches. Mom makes breakfast then she and the kids sit at the table together, eat, and enjoy each other's company. Dinnertime at the Gregorys' finds everyone in the family taking turns cooking, doing dishes, feeding the pets, and sweeping the floor. The person who cooks picks the menu for that meal so all family members can have their favorite dish one night a week.

On laundry day Mom does all the wash except Dad's, which he prefers to do himself. The kids fold the clothes, and everyone helps put them away. On weekends the family works in the yard together dividing up the mowing, trimming, fertilizing, and other chores. They also have a tradition called "Big Cleaning Day," where each family member dusts, scrubs, vacuums, etc. two rooms of the house. In an hour, the entire house sparkles.

Household chores look a little different at the Perez house, where dad and his two teenage sons live together during the week. Dad leaves a list of chores for the boys to complete before he gets home from work. The boys suggested this method. It was also their idea to choose items from the list and to do them on their own time schedule. They agreed that if they haven't finished their chores before Dad gets home, they will do them immediately if he has to say anything.

When Mr. Perez first told the boys he was going to leave a list of chores for them to do, he met with resistance. When he asked them what they thought would work, to his surprise they suggested almost the identical idea. Mr. Perez isn't the first parent to fail at getting cooperation by giving orders and to succeed when he invited his children to help solve the problem.

The Nakamuras have four children, all involved in sports programs. Leaving lists was hopeless because no one was ever home to complete the chores on the list. When the parents scolded and criticized, the children rebelled, saying they were too busy with practices and games to help.

When Mom and Dad asked the children to help figure out a way to get work done that was fair for the family, the kids responded with great ideas. No one in the family thought it was fair for only one person to do all the work. The children knew intimately about teamwork and fair play from their athletic experiences. They were willing to help the family if they could find jobs that didn't need to be done daily. The family brainstormed a list of possibilities.

The oldest boy got excited about being in charge of organizing the garage. He agreed to spend one day a month on that chore. He works with his radio tuned to a sporting event while he arranges the shelves and puts away the items everyone deposits on the garage floor during the month. The two youngest children thought it would be fun to work with their father one day each weekend, shopping and making sandwiches for everyone's weekday lunches. They created an assembly line and froze bags of sandwiches labeled Monday, Tuesday, etc. for each family member. The second child volunteered to grocery shop with Mom, and on days he was home, he would set the table and empty the dishwasher. With all this help, Mom and Dad were glad to complete the daily chores.

Some families have sophisticated systems for chores. Others have less formal procedures. The Murdock household has six children—his, hers, and ours. Since not all of the children are at the house on the same days, assigning chores, making lists, and holding family meetings did not work. One day, in desperation, Mrs. Murdock took out a lunch bag and decorated the front with these words: *Look inside for ways to help the family—Pick two.* Then she filled the bag with chore suggestions on separate slips of paper, set the bag on the kitchen table, and went about her business.

The youngest children were the most curious and soon pulled slips from the bag. They couldn't read so they found a parent or older sibling to tell them what was on the paper. Soon everyone was pulling slips out of the bag, looking for something he or she liked doing. Amazingly, this simple system has worked for several years.

These families are social pioneers. They wanted to do things differently and were willing to find a system that worked. Sometimes things got worse before they got better, but the

family members were committed to making changes. Because of their creativity and willingness to try again and again, they persevered, sometimes through tears and tantrums.

Progress may be one step backward and three steps forward, but it is well worth the effort. To maximize your forward motion, we suggest you start by reading this entire book instead of only those sections that apply to your specific problems. If you can't immediately figure out how an idea fits your special circumstances, use your imagination and creativity to modify the information.

You will find many ideas for improving cooperation and changing negative energy into positive action in *Chores Without Wars*. We know these ideas work because we spent years developing and using them in our families and with our clients. As you read the following notes from each of us, you'll get a sense of how we came to write this book and why cooperation in the home is so important to us.

Notes from Lynn

When I was growing up, families in my neighborhood looked a lot alike. They usually had two parents and three or more children. The dads went off to work, and the moms stayed home, took care of the children, cleaned the house, and drank coffee with their friends. Moms nagged the children to clean their rooms, pick up their messes, and stop making more work. From a child's point of view, being a mom didn't seem like much fun—just a lot of work with little satisfaction.

When I became a mom, I didn't want to fall into the traditional role, nor did I want my children to think that only men worked at jobs outside the home and women always did the work inside the home. Yet in no time at all, I was following my mother's example. Fortunately, in 1969 a friend gave me Rudolf Dreikurs's book *Children: The Challenge*,[1] and I started to see ways to create a different world for myself and for my children.

Because I wanted to help my children feel useful, involved, and capable, I created simple opportunities for them to help the family. They enjoyed watering plants (even if much of the water ended up on the table), emptying silverware from the dishwasher, and deciding how to arrange salad on a plate. They felt successful wiping up a spill or breaking eggs into a bowl on baking day. Since they had no preconceived picture of how a family should act, they grew up assuming that in a family, everyone helps. I'll never forget my nine-year-old son coming home from dinner at a friend's house and sharing, "It was so weird! The mom cooked the meal, set the table, served the food, and did the cleanup all by herself. Did you know there were families like that?!"

---

1. Rudolf Dreikurs, *Children: The Challenge* (New York: E. P. Dutton, 1987).

It wasn't so easy to convince my husband that housework could be shared by all. When I began teaching parenting classes, I found that men weren't alone in having a hard time changing their picture of how a family should operate. Anyone with a traditional picture found changing difficult—women and children included.

Since many of my clients and friends struggled with the same issues, I invited two colleagues who were also making family changes to write a book with me to help families work cooperatively. Riki Intner, Marilyn Kentz, and I published *Family Work: Whose Job Is It?* Countless families used our ideas to bring about shared decision making and peaceful relationships in their homes.

But families are changing and so are their needs. The folks at Prima Publishing recognize this and are interested in helping families find ways to take the drudge out of chores, make work in the family a harmonious, cooperative venture, and build skills for all family members. They invited us to revise our material and publish our book under the DEVELOPING CAPABLE PEOPLE SERIES imprint with a new title, *Chores Without Wars*.

Since we wrote our first book, we have worked as speakers, parent educators, and family therapists. We have used the book ideas in our counseling business, with parents in recovery, and in school classrooms. In addition, I have experienced many variations in my family composition. Ours became a mixed household when my children's friends lived with us temporarily, a single-parent household after divorce, a blended household following remarriage, and it has recently become an adults-only household. I welcome the opportunity to share what these experiences taught me about creating cooperative households.

Notes from Riki

I grew up with a pretty traditional view of families. My dad went off to work each day. My mother stayed home and ran the house. I went off to school and was responsible for keeping my things picked up and straightening my bed at home. If I cooked or baked, I had to clean up and leave the kitchen as I found it. I didn't think much about laundry, shopping, cooking, and cleaning. Most of the families around functioned as ours did.

When I got married, both my husband and I had full-time jobs and worked together to clean up around the house. But I did the cooking, shopping, and laundry, while he looked after the car. We lived in a city apartment so had no garden or lawn to take care of. Once we started our family, we "fell" into the traditional model: he worked outside the home; I managed the household and children. We never talked or even thought much about it . . . until a few years later.

I had gone back to school, was working part time, and was still running our household and caring for our three children. Clean for five, shop for five, cook for five, wash for five. I felt like I was playing catch-up all the time and was tired of being "supermom." Fortunately I had gotten involved in parenting classes and began to realize my doing it all was making me feel resentful, robbing my children of opportunities to feel useful and capable, and eliminating chances for us to cooperate as a family. I learned about routines and began to create ways for everyone to develop skills and be involved in the tasks that made our family work.

At first my family was not enthusiastic about the changes, but with patience, support, and perseverance, over time we all experienced benefits from our efforts. We also grew to appreciate each other more.

After I had taught the topic "Family Work" at a drop-in parenting program, Lynn, Marilyn Kentz, and I got together to write down our ideas and share them with other families. *Family Work: Whose Job Is It?* was the result. That was in 1985. Since then we've learned more, seen our perspective and attitudes change, and watched new family configurations evolve. Prima Publishing recognizes how important it is for people to live together cooperatively. They encouraged us to revise our materials, and *Chores Without Wars* is the result.

CHAPTER 1

Creating a Cooperative Family: Getting Started

Use your imagination for a moment, and pretend you live in a home with a full staff of servants. They cook for you, clean for you, entertain you, and spend most of their energy making your life as pleasant as possible. All of a sudden, for no apparent reason, they quit. They inform you they'll continue to do some things, but from now on, you'll be expected to pitch in and help. You certainly wouldn't jump up and down with glee saying, "Oh thank you, thank you for not doing everything for me anymore!" Instead, you'd be shocked, angry, scared, and determined to get them back in your service, or hire new servants.

If you've been "a full staff of servants" for your family members, this fabrication may help you imagine their reaction to sudden change. Even though the tips in this chapter can make the job of winning family cooperation easier, your household members may be in shock. Expect changing old patterns to take time. Set no finish line, since creating a cooperative household is a continuous, evolving process. It's normal to want things to change immediately, but some changes seem to take forever while others occur as if by magic.

Even if you are fortunate enough to have a highly motivated group of people in your family, the transition will still be gradual. But a lack of cooperation in your family can make the

11

difference between peace or hostility. If you aren't sure whether your family is cooperative or resistant, the following list can serve as a reality check.

Seven Signs of a Lack of Cooperation

1. **Unresolved grievances.** It is unlikely that people who share a household have the same daily living habits. Some people like the TV or radio on for background noise and others can't stand anything but complete silence. Some people squeeze the toothpaste in the middle; others squeeze the tube at the end. Rarely do two people have the same standards for cleanliness. But if such gripes become sources of constant irritation without hope of resolution, they can tear households apart.

2. **Constant complaints.** "That's not fair! I have to do everything around here." "You never keep your promises." "Stop acting like my mother." "That's a man's (woman's) job, so I'm not going to do it." Do any of these complaints sound familiar? They are signs of building resentment. If unheeded, they soon escalate and erode relationships.

3. Imbalance in work distribution. One person often decides that it's less hassle to do what needs to be done than to argue, nag, or put up with the chaos. A feeling of hopelessness often leads to the decision to do more than a fair share. Taking on too much demonstrates both lack of self-respect and lack of respect for others. Family members lose out on opportunities to contribute and build skills when everything is done for them. One person's overdoing is also a sign that other family members are willing to take advantage, consciously or unconsciously, of the household member who has the lowest tolerance for certain forms of chaos.

4. Arbitrary assignment of responsibilities (by age, sex, or other categories). Operating by assumptions instead of agreements create no-win situations in a household. Just because someone's mother cleaned the windows and attended to the inside of the house while the father organized the garage and took care of the outside chores doesn't mean there are no alternatives. If someone insists that his or her way is the only way or the right way, that person is being arbitrary and closed-minded instead of cooperative.

5. Conflict avoidance. Every household has things family members disagree about. Thinking problems will go away by themselves is a delusion. The result of this "magical thinking" is putting up with feelings of irritation, aggravation, and anger instead of practicing problem solving. Avoiding conflict by saying nothing leads to more serious friction in the family. Since family members aren't mind readers, they can't work together to solve problems unless they know what the problems are.

6. Yelling, threatening, nagging, bribing, coercing. These behaviors inhibit cooperation and if they are the primary tools for gaining assistance, they will result in rebellion and passive resistance. Family members may say yes with their words but no with their actions by not following through. A rash of forgetfulness or an abundance of promises to do a job later may mean that someone in the family is using motivational methods that invite undesirable behaviors instead of enlisting cooperation.

7. **Blaming and fault finding.** Looking for blame and finding fault are sidetracks to real problem solving. Family members feel hurt and picked on when others attack them instead of attacking the problem.

If you recognize any of the seven signs of a lack of cooperation in your family and you are ready to change how work gets done in your household, start by evaluating your attitude. What are your beliefs about who is supposed to do a job, about how long changes take, and about how to motivate others? Your attitude, expectations, and style will make a tremendous difference in whether you succeed or fail.

Examine and Change Your Attitude About Who Is Responsible

It is not unusual for family members to maintain traditional values that interfere with their making changes. Values are unconscious decisions all of us made as young children about the way we think things are supposed to be. Value decisions are usually black-and-white decisions about what we think is right or wrong, good or bad. Since we made these basic decisions before we were five, we were unaware that we were deciding. We believed that what was happening in our families was how the world should be. As we got older and were confronted with new perceptions and experiences that challenged our value systems, we were reluctant to do anything different. Values (beliefs about the way things should be) are the last things we change.

If you grew up with traditional values and still believe that there are separate and definite roles for men, women, and children to fulfill, you probably won't welcome someone telling you that times have changed and you have to change. If you believe that men are the "breadwinners" and women are the "homemakers," trying something different may seem as impossible as trying to convince an energetic four-year-old that he or she still needs a nap.

If you were expected to do as you were told when growing up, you probably expect your children to do as they are told now. If jobs were assigned by your parents who told you what to do, you may find it strange to sit down with your children and make decisions about household responsibilities together. If your parents told you to go out and play and not to worry about work until you got older, you were probably left with the idea that work is a burden and helping the family is a drudge—or someone else's job. Are you sending that same message to your children?

If your family divided chores by sex, age, or some other arbitrary method when you were growing up, you may find it difficult to let go of the old assumption of how it "should be done." Many women feel guilty asking for help or not doing all the work inside the home like their mothers used to. In spite of their resentment, they feel uncomfortable stepping out of their traditional role of being in charge of home and hearth. They have no model or picture that shows them how to include their partner or children without feeling guilty. At the same time, women are often afraid to give up the power that comes with managing their homes. They are also reluctant to involve their spouses and children as they haven't yet learned how to include others in day-to-day decision making and household management.

Men often believe that their working outside the home to earn a living is sufficient contribution to the family. Unfortunately, many men continue to believe this even when their wives also work outside the home. Even when both parents work outside the home, the old values are hard to shake, often leaving one family member to struggle alone to keep up with the endless tasks necessary to maintain the household.

If you recognize such values in yourself or think your job is to do everything, begin by telling yourself that helping with work around the house is everybody's job. Everyone who is part of the problem must be part of the solution. That includes dads, moms, grandparents, little kids, big kids, roommates, and anyone else who is part of the household. To succeed, you may have to reevaluate your expectations.

Create Realistic Expectations

Do you expect to get things organized in a week or so? Dream on! Do you think that when people agree to do certain tasks, they'll automatically remember without slipups or reminding? Such expectations are sure to set you up for disappointment and failure. If you have unrealistic expectations, you may give up too easily and go back to the old ways of doing things.

Try an experiment. Fold your hands. Look down and see which thumb is on top. Now refold your hands and put the opposite thumb on top. Hold that position as long as you can. Notice the discomfort and how much you want to go back to your original position. That's how hard it is to change. Give yourself and your family members a break. It's hard to make changes . . . even for you.

Sally Kroller is a good example of a parent with unrealistic expectations. She insisted her family meet with her counselor to get them to help out at home. During the counseling session, everyone reluctantly agreed to do two chores each day. The next day Sally came home from work expecting to see the chores done but walked into a disaster area instead. In a rage, she stood in front of the TV set and yelled.

"Look at this mess. I've been at work all day and I come home to toys, shoes, and magazines all over the living room floor. When you were at the counselor's, you agreed to pick up each day. Look at this mess! There are dirty dishes in the living room and piles of clean laundry on the sofa. I suppose you're waiting for me to fold everything. You told the counselor you would help, and now you aren't keeping your promises. Gary, is that your dirty laundry? . . . What have you been doing all day? No one cares about me!"

If Sally Kroller wants to live in a family where people ask, "What can I do to help," she needs to reevaluate her attitude about perfection and justice. When she judges progress by how smoothly the family runs or how quickly family members change, she discourages herself and others. Sally can help her family succeed by having more reasonable expectations and taking smaller steps. She can suggest that family members choose a work time when everyone works together for ten to fifteen minutes each day. Once her family gets into the routine of helping, they will be more likely to keep their agreements without being prodded or scolded.

It is more realistic to view change as a process and to focus on progress instead of perfection. Instead of measuring success by the results like Sally did, work to create a cooperative family, not just a clean living room. Rather than trying to divide chores equally, look for ways to start where the entire family can experience some success. Success builds success. Start with small steps and celebrate improvement. When you build on these small steps, you'll soon have big accomplishments.

Don't Let the Initial Resistance To Change Stop You

It is normal to experience resistance to change, even if you follow all the suggestions in *Chores Without Wars*. Attitudes vary among household members. Some in the family may be highly motivated to change while others resist change at any cost. Ideally, family members will want to help each other put a respectful, cooperative system in place. If that isn't the case, the change process may take longer, but all it takes is one person committed to making changes to get things started.

In many family situations, members who participate the least feel the most threatened by the change. These family members worry that the changes will place an extra burden on them and may think, "If I start helping with one thing, there may be no end to the demands to do more. Besides working full time, I'll have to do all the housework, too." Inexperienced workers may fear looking stupid because they believe they should know how to do the job already. Some may have a hard time fitting in the extra jobs while others may resist giving up their free time.

When family members who previously did most of the family work delegate, they may enjoy the help at first, but later worry that others won't do the jobs correctly. They resist suggestions to hire work out because they want everyone to experience doing some of the work. Sometimes they struggle with their identity, thinking they are worthwhile only when they are the helpful, responsible, capable member of the family. At first, family members who once did most of the chores may feel lost and guilty relaxing. It's hard for those used to doing something all the time to put their feet up, read a book, go for a walk, talk to a friend, or take time to smell the flowers.

Children see helping as a game at first, but later, as they realize helping is "a way of life," the jobs become a burden. If children have gotten used to parents providing "maid," "janitorial," or "restaurant" service, they miss this when it's gone. Many children welcome the chance to have more say, but view their new responsibilities as a loss of freedom.

The Clawsons were a case in point. When Ellen Clawson came home from her parenting class requesting more help from the family, her husband Mike was the first to say, "I'm not doing housework. You're home all day; it's your job." The three children, following Dad's lead, chimed in, "Dad's right. You're the mom. It's your job." She remembered her instructor telling the group that people are often initially resistant to change, so she was ready for this. Instead of feeling put off or arguing, she asked the family if they would be willing to continue discussing their feelings after dessert.

Before she began to clear the table after dinner, she said, "Tell me more about why you think it's up to me to do all the work around the house. Are there reasons other than the fact that I'm the mother or that I'm home during the day? I'd like to hear your thoughts." Four-year-old Max spoke up first. "Mom, I don't know how to cook or clean." Everyone laughed.

Then eight-year-old Kevin said, "All my friends' moms stay home and take care of everyone. Why can't you be like other moms? And what if my friends came over and saw me doing dishes? That's girls' work."

"I don't have time to do any jobs at home. I'm trying to keep my grades up, I'm on the volleyball team, and my boyfriend is already complaining that he never gets to see me," said sixteen-year-old Jill.

"No wonder you're worried about changing things around here," Mom replied. "Let me ask you a question. Do you think it's fair for one person to do all the work? Would you like to be that person?"

"Ellen," said Mike, "we aren't trying to be unfair, but you *are* home all day."

Rather than getting angry or defensive, Ellen responded calmly: "I can hear all the reasons it would be hard to change. Maybe if we start by listing all the jobs that need to be done, it would be easier to see why I'm asking for help. I'm not suggesting that we divide up all the jobs equally, but I do have a lot of faith in our family and know we can come up with a solution that works for everyone."

The family agreed to make a list of jobs, and when they saw the length of the list, everyone offered to pitch in and help with at least one chore. Ellen knew this was a good beginning and she thanked her family for their understanding and their help.

Notice Your Style:
Do You Create Allies or Enemies?

Involving family members in family chores helps them learn how to plan, organize their time, juggle multiple projects, work in a give-and-take manner, be part of a team, and learn from mistakes. Ellen wanted her family to have a "can-do, we're in this together" attitude, and her discussion with the family was the beginning of a process to create that. She decided to focus on small steps and practice mutual respect. She listened to her family members' issues without arguing or getting defensive, but she held her ground and respected herself enough to give up her traditional role and help the family find a win/win first step.

Ellen Clawson's leadership style invited allies. Even though Ellen was doing more than her share in the household, she didn't let her feelings of anger or resentment get in her way. Instead of continuing to wait on everyone or complaining about her life, she became a coach and an organizer. She set realistic expectations because she knew that learning new skills takes time and planning. Because she focused on making changes step by step to win cooperation, she met with success.

Her neighbor, Beth Miller, had a different style. Beth noticed the changes taking place at Ellen's house and decided to try making a few changes with her own family. Beth, however, made serious mistakes by alternating between overcontrol and giving up.

Beth was always picking up after her nine-year-old twins, Brett and Bryce, and reminding them to do their chores. She had given up hope that her husband Harry would ever do anything inside the house. He told her that he would go to work every day and take care of the yard and the car on weekends; the house and the kids were her job. As Harry told her, "That's the way my parents did it, and that's the way it will be in my family." Beth had a traditional upbringing as well, so she resigned herself to the fact that this was the way it would be. Still, she found herself tired and resentful by the end of most days.

Beth decided that even though Harry was unwilling to change, she could get the twins to help. She started by thinking of things the boys could do to pitch in. That afternoon, when Brett and Bryce came home from school, Beth told them she was tired of doing everything around the house, so they were going to have to start folding their laundry and doing the dishes. They both groaned. She delivered their clean clothes to their room and said, "Remember what I told you boys? Get these folded." They looked up but continued playing.

After dinner Beth stacked the dirty dishes at the sink and noticed the twins watching TV with Harry. "Boys, get in here and do these dishes," she called.

"As soon as this show is over. We always watch it."

An hour later the boys were still in front of the TV with their Dad and the dishes still were not done. "You boys didn't do the dishes!" Beth yelled. "You said just one show. Get in the kitchen right now!"

"We have to do our homework," they replied.

"Beth," Harry yelled, "stop making a fuss over the dishes. What's more important anyway, homework or a few stupid dirty plates?" Beth, feeling exasperated and defeated, went into the kitchen and started on the dishes.

Later that night when Beth went to tuck the boys in, she found their laundry basket overturned and the clean and dirty clothes mixed together. "I give up," she thought as she put all the clothes in the basket and carried it to the washing machine. "They'll never change!"

Think about the differences between Ellen's and Beth's actions. While Ellen invited her family members to share their thoughts and become involved in deciding what changes would be made, Beth announced to her children what they would do. Ellen didn't give in to others' views of how things should be, nor did she expect others to automatically accept hers. Instead, by inviting cooperation she helped the family find small steps everyone could live with and gathered allies.

Beth gave up on her husband without even trying to involve him. She tried to change too quickly, and when things didn't work, she gave up in exasperation instead of learning from her mistakes and trying again. As a result of trying to make others change then giving up on them completely, Beth created enemies.

What is your style? If you aren't sure, try an experiment. Look in a mirror and make the angriest face you can. Next make the biggest smile you can. Which face do you prefer looking at? Which face has the best possibility of winning cooperation? You can choose whether to smile or not. If you are getting bogged down by being too serious and forgetting to look for the humor in each situation, try smiling to change your attitude. It's hard to stay serious with a smile on your face.

Even with the most positive attitude, realistic expectations, and collaborative style, making changes can still be difficult. Following the suggestions in *Chores Without Wars* will help your family find respectful ways to work with each other and learn how to live together in peace and harmony.

CHAPTER 2

Implementing Eight Practical Pointers to Accelerate Change

It's never too early or too late to get your family working together. By implementing the eight practical pointers in this chapter, you can help family members like themselves and each other, cooperate with each other, and take responsibility for their own behavior. Practicing respect for self and others makes implementing changes easier and helps family members (including you) break bad habits. Trying to change others slows down the process of working together; changing yourself accelerates cooperation. A small alteration on your part can bring about monumental changes in others. In this chapter, we offer eight pointers to help you change yourself that simultaneously invite cooperation from others.

1. Focus on One Thing at a Time and Practice the New Habit Until It Becomes Routine

Start by choosing one task to concentrate on for a week. Retraining yourself and the rest of your family is easier when you work on one thing at a time. Trying to accomplish too much at once overwhelms everyone. Since making lasting changes requires focus and concentration, pick a time when you aren't distracted to practice new habits and practice for at least a week before you change the plan, add to it, or throw it out.

Gretchen, a twenty-five-year-old graduate student living with three other friends, was upset with the lack of cooperation in her household. When she complained, her roommates said they were tired of Gretchen's whining and demanding tone. Gretchen said, "If you pitched in, I probably wouldn't sound so awful." Gretchen wanted her friends to change, but her efforts were failing.

One day Gretchen accidentally recorded herself complaining about the messes. Shocked at the nagging tone in her own voice, she decided to practice five minutes a day using a more pleasant tone. She recorded herself during her practice time and listened to the tape in her car on the way to work. In less than a week, her roommates noticed the difference and commented on how much nicer it was to be with Gretchen.

In another household, Steve, a single parent of two school-age children, was constantly irritated and resentful because his children acted like guests in the house. Instead of talking about this with his children, he kept doing everything himself. To change this pattern he decided to ask for what he wanted and say how he felt for thirty minutes each day.

That evening, he set the timer on the stove for a half hour before dinner, he said to his eight-year-old son, "Hey, Blake, I want some help with dinner. How about setting the table?"

"No way, Dad, I'm right in the middle of Super Mario Brothers."

"Blake, I don't like being treated like a servant. Lissie, how about you? Will you set the table or do some other job to get dinner started?"

Ten-year-old Lissie stared wide-eyed at Dad and said, "I thought you liked doing everything yourself. I didn't know you were angry. Why didn't you just ask for help?"

Steve, in shock, answered, "I thought I had."

"No, Dad, you didn't. If you ask in a nice voice, I'll help you."

After a week of practicing openness, Steve was amazed at how much Lissie was involved in family routines. Even Blake was turning his game off and watching his father and his sister. Steve decided it was worth continuing his new behavior for another week to see what would happen. He also noticed that he wasn't as angry and was actually enjoying spending time with the children.

You don't have to change everything at once. By focusing on one thing at a time, like Steve did, you can relax, knowing that you and your family are gradually learning new ways to relate, step by step.

2. Act Without Talking

The most important way you can improve cooperation at home is to talk less and act more. Watch parents at the mall, the grocery store, or the park. Listen to how many words they use while trying to motivate their children. Not only do they give countless orders, but they point out their own failure to motivate by saying, "If I told you once, I told you a thousand times." Children respond to this verbal deluge by tuning it out.

If you say things over and over or give long explanations or lectures, you're talking too much. If you're trying to motivate your kids with threats or yelling, you'll be ineffective. If you notice your children holding their hands over their ears or getting a glazed look in their eyes, these are clues that you are talking too much.

Talk less and act more. Don't speak unless you think first. Ask yourself, "Do I really mean what I am about to say? If I mean it, am I willing to follow through with action? Am I requesting something that is possible?" If the answer to any of these questions is no, don't talk.

Once you do say something, be ready to act. Action is more likely if you're standing up, so stand before you start talking. That way, if action is needed, you're halfway there.

Perhaps one of your children agreed to do a job but hasn't done it. Instead of yelling from another room, get up, go to the child, stand where you have eye contact, and say once, "You need to empty the garbage" (or whatever). The rest is up to the child. Don't argue or explain. Just stand quietly and wait. Try it! The results can be amazing.

Lead a younger child by the hand to a task, keeping your mouth closed rather than shouting directions from another room or talking as you go. If it's time for dinner, walk to your child, take his or her hand, and *gently* pull. If the child resists, don't let go of his or her hand, but do let up the pressure and move toward him or her. When the child stops pulling in the other direction, try again. It only takes a couple of gentle tugs to let your child know it is time to go.

You might also practice acting without talking by leaving certain jobs undone and allowing family members to experience the results. For instance, instead of chasing down kids or clothes when the dirty clothes aren't in the laundry, you might wash only the ones in the hamper. If toys aren't picked up by a certain time, you might put them in a box on a high shelf until the weekend.

Tell your children in advance what your plan is. Make sure you have their undivided attention then *say it once!* After that, just *act.* If family members have issues with your plan, arrange a family meeting to discuss how each person feels about what happened and what needs to be done. (See more on Family Meetings in Chapter 5.)

Mrs. Singh was eager to try acting more and talking less. Tired of hassling with her children when it was time to go places in the car, she sat her three boys down and said, "Boys, from now on, I'll let you know ten minutes before it's time to leave and I'll set the timer on the stove. When the timer goes off, I'll be out the door and on my way with no reminders and no nagging. I know you three can help out if you want to."

"Okay, Mom. Can we go play now?" piped up the youngest.

"Sure, no problem," the older ones added.

That afternoon, Mrs. Singh poked her head in the playroom door and said, "Boys, I'm setting the timer to leave for baseball practice in ten minutes." None of her sons looked up or stopped what they were doing. Without another word, she went to the kitchen and set the timer. When it buzzed, she stuck her head in the door and said, "Time to go" then walked to the car.

One of her sons ran after her saying his brothers weren't ready. Mrs. Singh just smiled and started the engine. Her son ran back into the house and soon returned with his brothers, who carried their jackets and shoes.

"Mom, you're supposed to remind us and wait for us!" they complained.

Mrs. Singh continued to smile as the boys put on their seatbelts and settled in. As she backed up the car, one of her sons commented to his brothers, "Mom sure is acting weird. I don't think she's going to wait for us anymore if we're not ready. We better listen for the timer next time."

Mrs. Singh's boys were learning a valuable lesson: when Mom (or another grown-up) talks, it's a good idea to listen. They took Mom seriously because she was serious. When you use fewer words, you have more energy to enjoy yourself and your family.

3. Offer Limited Choices

How often have you heard a mother say, "Johnny, pick your truck up. NOW!" only to get, "No, I won't" for a reply? When you command or demand that your children, spouses, or housemates do things according to *your* time schedule or precisely the way *you'd* do it, you set the stage for a conflict. When you ask questions like "Do you want to pick up your cleaning on the way home?" you're likely to get "No" for an answer. When family members believe they have no choices, they often end up in power struggles.

By offering limited choices, you can define the limits of a situation yet still provide freedom of choice within the boundaries. By saying, "Johnny, do you want to pick up your truck or your ball first?" you let Johnny know you expect the job will be done. But you also communicate that Johnny can choose which toy to begin with. It's important to keep choices simple and to the point. Here are some examples:

"Do you want to dust the table or the bookshelves?"

"Do you want to put the silverware or the plates on the table?"

"Do you want to put your toy on the top shelf or the bottom shelf?"

"Do you want to choose a job to help the family or shall I assign you one?"

Once you offer limited choices, you don't need to repeat them. After the words comes action. If a family member gives an unacceptable third alternative, it's okay to say, "I'm sorry, that's not one of the choices." If a family member is unhappy with the way decisions are made, suggest he or she write the complaint on a list to discuss at a family meeting. (See Chapter 5 for more on family meetings.)

Trixie King decided to use limited choices while teaching her daughter, Daphne, how to pick up her toys. Trixie chose the time for cleanup by giving Daphne a limited choice, "Do you think we should put the toys away before dinner or before bed?" Daphne chose before bed. A half hour before bedtime, Trixie followed through with action. She stopped her other activities, found her daughter, and said, "This is the time you chose to clean up the toys. Let's get started. I'll help you." Then she sat on the floor with Daphne, working when her daughter worked and stopping when she stopped.

Trixie practiced the same routine every day before bedtime for one week. The second week, she suggested Daphne was ready to put the toys away without help. She arranged a non-verbal signal with her daughter to remind her it was cleanup time, again giving Daphne a limited choice: "Should I set the timer to ring, point to a picture of a clock, or just say 'toys' when it's cleanup time?" Her daughter asked Trixie to point to the clock and say "toys."

Trixie eliminated nagging, reminding, and tantrums with this method. Once the plan was working, she asked her husband if he would like to take a turn following through. Although one parent can make a change alone, everyone benefits when the plan is a joint effort.

4. Operate by Agreements Instead of Assumptions

To make assumptions is to take others for granted. Decisions about what is proper or improper based on one person's values are less effective than those derived through everyone sharing ideas to find a solution that works for all. People feel disregarded when they are expected to do certain jobs in certain ways based on one person's assumptions.

Agreements involve eliciting opinions to find a harmonious plan of action. When everyone who is part of the problem is invited to be part of the solution, the guesswork is taken out of decision making. Agreements imply choice. When people know they have a choice and have agreed to the plan, they are more willing to carry it out. Operating by agreements is respectful. Operating by assumptions is disrespectful. Expecting the kids to do dishes because they are kids, men to empty garbage because that's a "man's job," or women to cook because that's a "woman's job" are examples of common assumptions. The following comments came from household members who did not like operating by others' assumptions.

"I'm sick of doing the outside work. Chopping firewood and planting a garden is a lot harder than dusting and doing dishes. How come the girls get to do the easier work inside?"

"I hate babysitting. I wish you never had my little sister!"

"I'm always buying the toilet paper around here. Do you guys think I'm your mother? It seems like I'm the only one who cares if this place is equipped."

When these household members decided to practice making decisions by agreements instead of assumptions, the result was cooperation. Once the family members knew they had options, they changed their outlooks. In the first scenario, the young man who expressed discontent about yard work changed his mind when someone suggested rotating jobs on a weekly basis. After giving it some thought, he said, "If no one minds, I'd rather stick with the outside work. I'm getting so used to it that I enjoy it."

The upset older sibling who felt put upon when expected to babysit said, "I'm sorry I said I wish you never had my sister. What I meant was I don't like just being expected to babysit. Ask me if I'd be willing to babysit first. Usually I'll say yes, but I want to know it's okay to say no when it's not convenient for me."

In the family with the toilet paper shortage, the house member who felt irritated and taken advantage of spoke up and told everyone. One of the housemates said, "We thought you were joking about the toilet paper. Now that we know you are serious, maybe we could come up with a plan. Why don't we take turns each week doing the shopping? If we're out of something, we could write it on a master list. If we started a fund for groceries we all use, the person in charge of shopping for the week could use that money to buy the things we share."

So many conflicts in a family go away when everyone knows there are choices. It is human nature to make assumptions, but that doesn't mean human nature can't be replaced by thoughtful, pro-active, and respectful behavior.

5. Watch Out for Pink and Blue Ribbons!

Stereotyping jobs by sex is one kind of assumption that leads to problems in a family. Boys can iron, do dishes, and fold clothes, and girls can wash cars, mow lawns, and empty garbage. Women can change the oil and men can cook dinner. Instead of "men's work" and "women's work," there's just "work that needs to be done."

It is equally disrespectful to arbitrarily insist that boys and men do jobs traditionally done by women, and vice versa, without family members having a say. We encourage you to help

your children learn how to do many different jobs. The more skills family members have, the better their lives work. Once family members master tasks, if they wish to switch with other members to do something they prefer, and the switch is mutually agreeable, we suggest you avoid getting hung up in male/female role issues.

If the family has used traditional role-stereotyping to divide jobs, changing may be difficult. When one mother overheard her child ask Dad to go shopping for shoes, she worried that the kids wouldn't need her anymore. In another family, the mother decided to take more responsibility for her own car. She watched her husband change the oil and thought it looked easy. She started the project and accidentally tightened instead of loosened the oil filter. Three hours later with the help of AAA, the job was finished. She decided to take a beginning car maintenance class at the junior college to help make the job easier.

Changes may not come easily, but making them is important. With the changes in society, it's best to prepare both your sons and daughters for life by getting rid of pink and blue ribbons for chores. The more your children learn while they live at home, the easier their lives on their own will be.

6. Prepare Your Younger Children To Help the Family

If you have several children, it's tempting to ask older ones to show younger ones how to do a job or to supervise and make sure a work activity gets done. We don't recommend this. The skills and patience needed to work with new learners are more likely to be found in adults. Older children get frustrated when younger brothers and sisters don't cooperate. They tend to be bossy and punitive, especially when they are afraid of getting in trouble for the job not getting done.

Spending time instructing your children is rewarding. You learn more about them—how they think and what motivates them—and your children enjoy the attention you give them.

Because training is time-consuming, parents can be supportive and helpful by sharing the load. It has been our experience that the parent who has traditionally been less involved is often the most effective when teaching new patterns, as there is less history of nagging and fighting with the children over jobs. This parent tends to talk less and act more; the children are more likely to listen and follow through.

7. Don't "Baby the Youngest"

Parents often underestimate the abilities of their youngest children, treating them as helpless and incapable and telling them to wait until they're older to help around the house. Older siblings may also discourage younger brothers and sisters by criticizing their work, jumping in to do the job first, or doing the job over. All children need a chance to be involved in household work to gain a sense of belonging, usefulness, and importance. There's plenty to go around, so make sure you don't leave someone out because of his or her age. Instead, go out of your way to think of jobs your youngest can perform to contribute and succeed at. (See pages 76–78 for age-appropriate suggestions). At the same time, ask your older children to step back and give the youngest a chance to learn and be capable.

Two-year-old Sophie continually said "Me help" when family members worked around the house. Everyone laughed and told her she could help by playing with her toys. Sophie's lower lip would quiver as she walked to her play area and picked up a toy. One day, her mother Nora noticed Sophie looking with fascination at the new dustbuster. "Sophie," Nora asked, "would you like to help Mommy clean today? I'll wash the windows while you vacuum the cat hair off the couch with our dustbuster."

Sophie grinned from ear to ear as she grabbed the vacuum.

"Here, honey, let me show you how it works," Nora added. "It's easy. First push the button and the dustbuster goes on. Then push it back and forth on the couch over the cat hairs. You try."

Sophie's expression turned serious as she pushed the button and moved the vacuum over the couch. "Me help, me help," she squealed with glee.

Nora realized two-year-old Sophie looked like a baby next to her five-year-old brother Sid and seven-year-old sister Patsy. Nora remembered that Patsy was a little over two when Sid was born. Patsy looked so big that Nora had counted on her to help with the new baby! Nora realized, with embarrassment and sadness, that the family was doing Sophie a disservice by treating her like a helpless baby.

When Nora shared this with the rest of the family, everyone agreed that it was time to involve Sophie in family chores. Since Sophie enjoyed using the dustbuster so much, her father remounted the vacuum in the closet at a height Sophie could reach. Whenever the cat hairs got too much or someone noticed crumbs on the floor, they called, "Sophie!" She came run-

ning, opened the closet, took down the dustbuster, turned on the switch, and cleaned up the mess.

Sometimes parents want younger children to pitch in, but the children insist they are too little. Don't fall for their discouragement or manipulation. Instead, find a small way to involve them. Instead of saying, "It's okay, you can help when you get older," try saying "Let's do this together. I'll hold one end while you hold the other" or "I'll hand you a dish and you carry it to the counter." Find ways they can successfully contribute rather than let your children learn they can make excuses and be exempt from helping the family.

8. Watch Out for Pity

You may sometimes feel protective of your older children, too. You want them to have a variety of experiences, to enjoy themselves, and to be happy. When your children get older, they become more involved with their friends and have more social commitments. Schoolwork and homework become more challenging, and there is more of it. When your children say "Do I have to do the dishes tonight? I have so much homework I'll never get it all done!" or "I'll do the lawn next week. All the kids are going to the movies and I don't want to miss out," it is tempting to feel sorry for them and take over their jobs.

When you feel sorry for your children and take on their household work, you show subtle disrespect for them by assuming your children can't handle more responsibility. You also show a lack of self-respect if you act on the assumption that it is your job to fix everyone's problems. You may end up feeling burdened and resentful.

Instead of feeling sorry for your children and taking on their tasks, suggest your family sit down together to discuss rescheduling household work or redistributing tasks. By working together to solve the problem, you can be flexible without letting older children think they are exempt from helping.

You can still do favors for other household members. In fact, we hope you will all help each other and practice give and take. But all family members need to realize that being busy is no excuse for placing extra burden on others or to assume that another should do your job.

By following the eight pointers in this chapter, you are on your way to a more cooperative household. These pointers lay the foundation for family members to take more personal responsibility. Everyone in the house will feel more capable as you practice the pointers. In the next four chapters, we suggest ways you can continue the growth process in your home with ideas for creating routines, tips on encouragement, suggestions on how to set up family meetings, and guidelines for establishing allowances.

CHAPTER 3

Making It Work: Developing an Encouraging Style

When your two-year-old "helps" you set the table and places the silverware upside down, or your three-year-old "helps" vacuum and covers only a small part of the room, or your husband leaves a gap sure to spring a leak when he diapers the baby, it's easy to say, "Here, I'll do that." If you criticize or take over, you discourage potential helpers.

Think how people behave when they feel confident, capable, and good about themselves. Remember the last time you felt on top of the world? Was there anything you couldn't do? When family members feel encouraged, there are few limits to what they can do.

Unfortunately, it's often difficult to encourage those around you if you didn't grow up feeling encouraged. Its natural to mimic the discouraging comments and looks you received as a child. When you notice that tasks aren't completed or done right, it's automatic to point out mistakes or halfhearted efforts. You focus on the negative, hoping to motivate others to do better. Instead of encouraging, you discourage others and invite them to do worse or not try at all.

The good news is that you can learn to be more encouraging. You can learn to think, act, and speak differently.

Respecting Different Ideas and Standards Means a Change in Your Thinking

When you get caught up in thinking yours is the right way, you can be especially discouraging to young children. Have you noticed how children resist cleaning their rooms? You may have created this "monster" by insisting they use your "right" way to clean their bedroom. When you focus on their progress instead of your picture of perfection, you get better results.

By shifting your attitude, you can enjoy your child's idea of a "clean" bedroom, where the bed is made (but full of lumps) and the floor is clean (the toys are pushed under the bed). If your children cleaned the room themselves and are proud of their work, focus on their enthusiasm and sense of accomplishment. You may even learn to love a lumpy bed!

If you persist in setting the standards, other problems will arise as your family works . . . unless you change your thinking. Your idea of "clean," "organized," or "straightened" may not be the same as another's. Honoring another person's way of

thinking can lead to creative new ideas and a sense of "our household."

When Joanie's boyfriend moved out and she needed help with the rent, she asked her friend Pam to move in. Pam had two young children and was excited to move from her apartment to a house. Joanie was careful to point out where things went and how she liked things. As a result, Pam had a hard time feeling like this was home.

Joanie came home one day to find that Pam had reorganized "her" kitchen. At first she was angry because the changes made it hard for her to function, but she soon realized that this drastic measure accomplished two important things: First, her new roommate's children were able to reach and find things more easily. Second, the ownership of the kitchen had changed from "Joanie's" to "the family's."

Pam also introduced some new cleaning products that worked better than Joanie's old ones. Her children wanted to try out the new product one of their friend's mothers used. They had such a good time making the bathtub sparkle after their bath that they asked if they could clean the tub and sink on cleaning day. Joanie realized that, by making room for new ideas, she was encouraging involvement.

Mr. Sawyer helped his wife consider a new strategy when he got involved in the grocery shopping. Mom and the kids had always divided the list at the store, even though it was difficult and bothersome. When Dad joined the family, he suggested dividing the list at home, where everyone could sit at the table and write down their items. This worked much better, and in no time, list making became a game, with everyone shouting out the items he or she wanted to find at the store. Instead of insisting there was only one way to do things, Mrs. Sawyer realized the benefits of changing her thinking.

Your attitude isn't the only thing that gets in the way of being encouraging. If you are constantly redoing others' work

or correcting them while they work, it won't take long before
they decide to stop helping. Your actions speak louder than
your words. If you say you want help, but redo everything
family members do, they can see you don't really mean what
you say.

Encouraging and Inviting Participation Through Your Actions

You have a decision to make. What is more important: having a
"perfect" house or encouraging family members to participate?
If you wish to be more encouraging, try the following:

- **Do Nothing and Bite Your Tongue**
  When one of the author's daughters was three, she volun-
  teered to help prepare for company by cleaning the toilet.
  After the company left, Mom went into the bathroom for
  the first time all night. To her dismay, the entire contents of
  the can of cleanser covered the bathroom in white powder.
  Her "gracious" guests had used the bathroom many times
  during the evening without saying a word.
- **Teach on the Fly**
  If you're cooking and your child says, "Can I help?" say
  "Yes!" and demonstrate how to crack an egg or stir the soup.
  When your roommate walks into the kitchen and asks what
  you're doing, show him how to use the pasta machine.
  When your wife says, I can't pound a nail in straight, hand
  her the hammer and say, "Go for it. Bent nails are easy to re-
  place."
- **Make It a Game**
  Emphasize the fun of work and make it a game whenever
  possible. Have a race putting things away, or set the timer
  and try to "beat the clock." Clean up papers by taking turns
  "shooting" them into the wastebasket. Pitch things into the

toybox from a few feet away. Write chores on pieces of paper and pick them out of a bag. Wear bathing suits to wash the cars and spray each other. Make an assembly line to pass dirty dishes to the sink.

- **Work Together**
  Schedule a "work time" when everyone is doing a job at the same time, even if each job is different. Try this when preparing dinner, doing yard work, cleaning up before bedtime, and preparing for holidays. A family of three decided to set aside a day for home improvements every six months. Between work days they kept a list of projects needing attention then tackled the list together on the chosen day.
- **Celebrate**
  Take instant pictures of family members standing next to a finished job. Start a scrapbook or display the pictures on the refrigerator or bulletin board. Have a barbecue or play a game when the household work is finished.

Changing your own actions goes a long way toward developing an encouraging style. So does changing your language.

Using the Language of Encouragement

Be aware that how you say things affects the direction you'll head. Your words may invite a result opposite from what you intend. If you think you're being encouraging, but household members rebel, check your language. In your effort to motivate, you may actually be discouraging them. How does this happen? To gain insight, look at the examples below to see if you inadvertently send the wrong message.

If You Say This	Others Hear
Let me do it!	You're not capable.
Go out and play.	Parents work, kids play.
You're too little.	You're not competent.
That's not the way.	You don't do things right.
Here, I can do that.	You're not capable of learning.
I don't do it this way.	You did it wrong.
You never do anything to help!	You're a bad person.

To develop an encouraging way of speaking, think about what you want to communicate. When you show respect and appreciation and focus on the efforts and improvements others make, you have a much better chance of sounding encouraging. Be glad that others are involved and let them know how much their help is appreciated. Then build on the successes you have. The following messages convey encouragement, promote cooperation, and instill confidence.

If You Say This	Others Hear
You try.	You're able to do things.
Here's the dustbuster so you can help!	Work can be enjoyable.
You can do it.	You're capable.

Thank you. That really helped.	Your help is appreciated.
What would happen if you add half a cup?	You're able to figure things out.
Cleanup time. Let's work together.	Everyone can contribute.
Let's do this together so it goes faster and we'll have time for a picnic.	We can help each other at work and play.

Words of encouragement focus on gratitude, appreciation, acceptance, effort, and uniqueness. At first it takes effort to think of encouraging things to say, but the results make the effort worthwhile.

Thinking, acting, and speaking positively also applies to fostering responsibility. You can prevent irresponsibility by having a positive, optimistic outlook. Telling yourself "They will" instead of "They won't" can create a positive outcome. Still, no matter how positive your attitude, agreements will be broken or forgotten at times. You can foster responsibility by using consequences instead of punishment at those times.

Using Natural and Logical Consequences

If a family member forgets a job, often a simple question like "What happened, I noticed the garbage is overflowing in the kitchen?" can get things back on track. Jobs not completed on a consistent basis indicate that you have a responsibility problem that needs attention. If the original plan was reasonable and realistic and you feel frustrated because the work is being done poorly or not done at all, it may be time to set up consequences.

One type is the natural consequence. Natural consequences allow people to find out what would happen if you did nothing. For instance, if one of your children "forgets" to set the table, you might call the family to dinner and say nothing.

The "forgetful" child would quickly remember he or she agreed to set the table.

If your roommate forgets she agreed to cook, you could read a book or watch TV as if nothing were wrong. As it got later, someone would get hungry and wonder about dinner. The key is to *do* and *say* nothing and allow the "forgetful" helper to experience the consequences of his or her behavior. Natural consequences are most effective with older kids and adults who might use chores as a battleground for fighting with you.

Sometimes using a "logical consequence" makes more sense. Let's say someone agreed to mow the lawn but "forgets." If you wait for the natural consequence and do nothing, you would watch the lawn turn to hay. If you are concerned about how the yard looks to the neighbors, a "logical consequence" might be more useful. You can say to the one responsible for mowing, "Not cutting the lawn when you've agreed to is not a choice. Since I'm unwilling to nag and remind, we need to decide on a consequence that will help you remember to cut the lawn as agreed. The consequence needs to be *related, reasonable,* and *respectful*.[1] Do you have any ideas? Let's brainstorm."

Choices might include . . .

- The lawn must be cut before dinner—no dinner until the lawn is cut.
- Work comes before play—TV and friends will have to wait until the lawn is mowed.
- Set up an inconvenient reminder in advance with your child—cut the lawn before the deadline or be inconvenienced and do it during a favorite TV show.
- Hire someone else to cut the lawn with the pay coming out of the child's funds.

Agree upon one choice and live with it for a week. Evaluate it at the end of an agreed-upon time period.

---

1. The "Three Rs of Logical Consequences" were first introduced by Jane Nelsen in *Positive Discipline* (New York: Ballantine Books, 1987).

Here is an example of a logical consequence one family used.

Mr. Carter couldn't understand why his wife had been unable to get their twelve-year-old son, Rory, to clean his room. His fourteen-year-old daughter, Amy, always put everything in its place, but Rory was impossible, littering his floor with clothes and toys. Mrs. Carter complained that she couldn't walk in Rory's room to get the laundry. She yelled and threatened, but the situation didn't improve.

After several weeks of attending a parenting class, Elaine was ready to tackle the problem in a new way. She talked with her husband and they agreed to meet with the children to discuss the problem. After Mr. and Mrs. Carter shared their views on the problem, Amy piped in, "But I always clean my room."

Mrs. Carter said, "Amy, we aren't looking for blame, just solutions. We need to come up with a plan we can all live with." Everyone shared ideas and both kids agreed to clean their rooms once a week. They all decided that if their room wasn't done before Sunday morning, they could not go anywhere or do anything until it was done.

The following Sunday morning Rory's friends came by to ask him to go bike-riding. When he asked his parents if he could go, they said, "Remember our agreement?" He told his friends he couldn't ride because he had work to do first. He was grumpy and sullen all day, but he did what he'd agreed to do. His parents knew the consequence itself was lesson enough so refrained from saying things like "Maybe next time you'll plan ahead!" or "Stop acting so grumpy; it's your own fault."

You may find that in spite of your best efforts, family members don't follow through. In such cases you can decide what you will (or will not) do in a situation and let the family know the consequences in advance. This is another form of logical consequences in which each family member has the choice of keeping the agreement or living with your consequence.

Margie Thompkins lived with her seven-year-old son, Lance. He agreed to pick up his toys each day. After a few weeks, Margie caught herself reminding Lance daily to pick up his toys. She told him that their plan wasn't working. Lance said, "I'll remember from now on. I'll pick up my toys."

Margie responded, "That's great. I'm glad to hear that, but I want to tell you what I've decided to do if you don't keep your agreement." Lance looked at her and asked, "What do you mean?"

In a friendly tone Margie said, "I'm not going to remind you or nag you anymore. I expect that you'll do what you say. If you haven't picked up your toys by 5:30 each evening, I'll figure you want me to do it. If I do it, I'll put the toys in a box called the 'Sunday Box,' and you can get them out the following Sunday."

The next few evenings Margie put a number of Lance's toys in the box. He started to scramble when he saw her putting his toys in the box. "I'm getting them," he shouted and raced around to pick them up. Margie noticed the floor was clear the next couple of nights and Lance was happy to get his toys back on Sunday. Although Lance left an occasional toy out after that, he usually had his toys picked up by 5:30 every day.

Logical consequences are most effective when children are young. Older family members often view consequences as punitive. You can improve this situation by letting them know what the problem is and asking for their help in solving it. By doing this, you may discover that the original plan is no longer realistic. For example, your teenage son may have agreed to take the garbage out on Tuesday nights but now has football practice that night. He gets home late and doesn't have time to do the job. He'd be willing to take the garbage out on Monday nights if you're willing to make the change.

If he still forgets, you might decide you are unwilling to make breakfast or to cook the next meal until the garbage is removed. Perhaps (with your son's agreement), you could seal the garbage bag and place it by the door to help him remember it's time to empty the garbage.

As you read the section on logical and natural consequences, you may have realized that you previously used the word "consequence" to mean punishment. If you think back to times someone punished you, you probably felt discouraged. It takes more time and creativity to find consequences that encourage rather than punish, but the result is cooperation and personal responsibility instead of intimidation or rebellion. We recommend one more way to change your thoughts, actions, and words so you can become even more encouraging to your family.

Using Birth Order Information To Encourage Others

The world looks different depending on your birth order. Rather than getting into the complexities of this fascinating subject, our goal is to show you ways to be more encouraging to children based on their birth order position. See the chart on pages 48–49 to help you in this effort.

Here's how one family used birth order information to encourage all their children to help with family work: Janet and Alvin Krasner have four children. Their oldest child, Tiffany, is twelve and is very responsible. She looks after the younger children and helps with the cooking, cleaning, and yard work. When the Krasner's started to include the younger children in the family chores, they saw a side of Tiffany they didn't know existed—she became critical, pouty, whiny, and angry. Janet and Alvin realized they had allowed Tiffany to take on too much responsibility, and the other children were acting less capable as a result.

Nine-year-old Jeffrey had convinced everyone that he was incapable of doing the chores, but after reading the Birth Order Chart, Janet realized that she had never spent any one-on-one time with him to show him how to do things. She set aside

Birth Order Chart

POSITION	TYPICAL CHARACTERISTICS	THINGS TO DO OR SAY TO BE ENCOURAGING
First Child	Wants to be first and best. Takes responsibility for other siblings. Likely to become a high achiever, responsible. Needs to feel right, perfect, superior—or gives up. Likes to be center of attention. Dethroned—becomes discouraged and problem. Protects, desires to be on top—superior.	Appreciate skills—"You're an expert at this." "This is your specialty." Avoid pressure to be perfect. Encourage the fun of participating, not the goal of winning.—"We're doing this together." Teach that "mistakes are for learning." Take time for training instead of assuming they have skills. Give choices. Ask to step back and let younger siblings do job. Pay for child-care.
Only Child	Used to being center of attention. Unsure of self in many ways. May feel incompetent compared to others. Likely to be responsible, achievement oriented. Often refuses to cooperate if fails to get own way.	Don't treat like slaves. Provide opportunities to work together with other children. Have spend-the-night company. Utilize child-care and nursery schools. Provide opportunities to participate instead of doing for them. Focus on effort—not perfection. Say, "I'm so glad you're helping," "I couldn't get it done alone," "Your help means a lot to me."
Second Child	Flexible and friendly. May try to catch up with older child's competence.	Encourage his or her own uniqueness. Avoid comparison with oldest. Tell them, "I need your help."

	Characteristics	Strategies
	May try to be older child's opposite in many ways. Not as concerned with rules. May rebel in order to find own place, feels life is unfair. Demands less attention	Solicit their input. Spend time one-on-one to teach skills.
Third Child	Squeezed—doesn't have the privileges of oldest or the prerogatives of youngest. May feel crowded out, unsure of position. May be sensitive, bitter, or revengeful. May be a good diplomat or mediator. Develops particular talent to distinguish themselves.	Make time for one-on-one work activities. Include in family work. Ask for his or her opinion: "How can we do this?" Listen and encourage them to share feelings. Ask to step back and let younger sibling handle tasks. Give appreciation—"You really helped," "You have good ideas."
Youngest Child	Often spoiled by parents and older siblings. Becomes the boss with their demands. Sometimes kept a baby. Does not learn skills. Often self-indulgent. May be highly creative. May be good at getting others to do things.	Do not do for the youngest (especially on a regular basis) what he or she can do alone. Don't rescue, don't pity. Say, "I know you can do this." Don't refer to as "the baby." Encourage self-reliance. Train to develop skills. Provide opportunities to participate. "Scale down" tools. Make it a game.

time to teach him how to fold the towels, wash lettuce in the spinner, and water the indoor plants. Jeffrey loved the special attention from his mother and was soon doing more work around the house. Whenever Tiffany saw Jeffrey helping out, she criticized and corrected him, but Jeffrey just said, "Mom showed me how to do it this way."

Six-year-old Monica disappeared whenever there was work to do. Alvin decided to help Monica be more capable. He started by asking for her help and for her opinion about how to do a particular job. "Honey," Alvin said, "do you think we should use the broom or the vacuum on the kitchen floor to pick up the dirt the dog dragged in?"

"I don't know, Daddy, because I've never cleaned the floor. Tiffany always does that job."

"Well, Tiffany has a lot to do around here, and it's time we helped her out. Why don't you get the vacuum and I'll get the broom and we'll try an experiment to see which one works best."

"Okay, Daddy, I'll be right back," Monica said, and ran to get the vacuum. Tiffany overheard this conversation in the next room and came running to her father in tears. "I thought cleaning the floor was my job. Don't you like the way I do it?"

Alvin gave Tiffany a big hug. "Tiffany, you do everything well, and we appreciate your help, but it's time for you to let your sister and brothers learn to help. There's plenty for all of us to do. You don't want Jeffrey, Monica, and Marcus to grow up and not know how to do things, do you?"

Tiffany thought for a minute. "You're right, Dad. It's time they learned, but I knew first!"

"You sure did, Tiffany, and you'll always be our very special daughter." Tiffany sniffed back her tears as she went back to her projects.

No one expected four-year-old Marcus to do a job well. Janet and Alvin asked the other children if they would be willing to stop calling Marcus their "baby brother" and to let Marcus work with them when a job needed to be done. When it was time to pick up the toys and dishes in the living room, a family member would call for Marcus, saying, "Marcus, we need your help. Come work with us to clean the living room." Marcus would come running, because he liked to be part of the family work. Janet found a chair Marcus could stand on and she taught him how to add ingredients to salads and to take the silverware from the dishwasher and put the pieces in the silverware drawer.

Janet and Alvin noticed Tiffany correcting her siblings or complaining about their work from time to time. They would wink at her and beckon her to them, whispering in her ear, "We love you, honey, and we appreciate you helping us help your sister and brothers grow up. Would you be willing to zip your lip and let them learn without criticism? I know it's hard, but we have faith in you."

Tiffany, feeling special for being her parents' ally, winked back and said, "Okay, I'll help you out."

Encouraging Yourself

If you are overwhelmed by the suggestions in this chapter, encourage yourself. Recognize your successes as you work. Remember, you'll get better at whatever you practice, so if you want to be more encouraging, keep practicing. The goal is not perfection but improvement. You will be happy to discover that, as you encourage others, you encourage yourself as well.

CHAPTER 4

Creating Security with Routines

Every household has routines. You may spend an hour trying to get your child to bed, night after night after night. In fact, you may sometimes feel like a trained lion jumping through a hoop as your child asks for another glass of water, just one more story, or a window shade adjustment to make the shadows on the wall go away. Doing the same thing over and over is a routine, but not the kind of routine that improves cooperation in a family . . . or the kind of routine we refer to in this book. If you resist the idea of routines and structure in your family, look at the unproductive routines you already have and consider replacing them with more positive options.

Everyone needs routines. Routines are like the guardrails at the cliff edge or the side of a bridge. Without guardrails, people are exposed to hazards and with them people can move freely and safely. Establishing routines creates security, a calmer atmosphere, and an opportunity to focus on what needs to be done. Instead of working because they've been ordered to, family members take responsibility for their behavior and work because it helps the family. Once the family creates routines, family members can choose to follow them, ignore them, or change them. Establishing routines offers an alternative to repeating ineffective patterns and an opportunity to create effective ones.

The earlier you start routines with young children, the more they think routines are just the way things are. Routines help eliminate power struggles and give all family members ways to belong and contribute to the family. Setting up routines takes five simple steps. By working on one problem at a time and following these steps to solve each, you can create a more relaxed atmosphere in your home.

Steps for Setting Up Routines

1. Discuss the problem any time other than when it is happening.
2. Involve everyone who is part of the problem to find a solution.
3. Use visuals (charts, lists, timer) as reminders of the plan.
4. Allow time for training and practice.
5. Follow the plan for a limited time. Review and change it only when family members meet together (a family meeting is a good time for this).

Here's how you might use these steps to help your children dress for school without your assistance.

Step 1.   Sit down with your children after school and tell them you'd like their help in setting up a new morning routine. You might start by saying, "I noticed you're getting better at doing things for yourself and you're old enough to get dressed without my help in the mornings."

Step 2.   Ask the children, "Do you have ideas that would help you get dressed on time without my reminding you?"
Listen to their ideas and offer your suggestions. If the children can't think of anything, you might propose something like the following:

"Do you want to lay out your clothes the night before or pick them out in the morning?"

"Would you like me to call you when breakfast is ready, or shall we set a timer?"

"If you come to the table undressed, would you like me to turn your plate upside down as a reminder to go finish or should I just tell you?"

Step 3. After agreeing with the children on a plan, depending on their ages, ask someone to write it down then post it on the refrigerator. Or find pictures in magazines of children getting dressed while the parents do other things and hang the pictures where everyone can see them. Suggest that you try out one idea for a week and plan a time to talk about how well the new routine is working at the end of the week.

For young children, charts can be amusing nonverbal reminders of routines. When it's work time, the chart instead of a nagging parent can help them remember. Mom or Dad might say, "Look at the chart and see whose turn it is to feed the dog." By showing each person's part, a chart also demonstrates vividly that everyone is part of the whole effort. Job charts should be simple and contain pictures. If the kids can help make them, all the better.

The chart on page 56 is used by one family of four to assign jobs to be done before dinner. It can be made with two paper plates, one with magazine cutout pictures and a larger one with family members' names. A round head fastener in the center allows the chart to be rotated daily or weekly.

Step 4. Spend the rest of the week practicing the plan. We call this "time for training." Do not remind or nag your children. Let them remember the agreement on their own. Your job is to simply follow through with your part of the plan. If you said you would turn their plate over if they came to breakfast without getting dressed first, do that. If your child asks you to give him or her another chance "just this once," say, "What was our agreement?" If your child can't remember the

plan, ask him or her to look at the picture chart or written agreement.

When children have taken part in making an agreement, they usually follow through. But practice time is necessary so the new routine becomes habit. During training time, don't add more suggestions or make changes. If you notice something that needs improvement, wait to see whether the problem corrects itself or discuss it at your next meeting.

As you begin, children need direction from you. As they gain more work experience, work along with them. Then pull back, staying nearby if needed.

Step 5.   At the next family meeting or at the end of a week, sit down with the children to discuss how the changes are going. Ask if they want to add or subtract parts of the plan. Perhaps you noticed the children wore clothing unsuitable for the weather. You might suggest packing away seasonal clothing. If your children want you to help pick out matching clothing, be willing to give them advice but encourage them to make the decision and let them learn from mistakes. Don't worry what people will say about you if your children wear unmatched clothing or fail to conform to your sense of style. Instead, remember children feel good when they have a sense of power, which can come from deciding what to wear.

After reevaluating the plan, go back to Steps 3 and 4 and try for another week. It may take a month or more to establish this routine. Don't start on a new problem until you feel comfortable that this one is solved.

Simplifying Routines

With young children, you can simplify the process of setting up routines by taking a leadership role and making work part of the daily schedule. You might say, "In our house we put away our toys before dinner," or "It's time for bath." If your children resist, let them know you'd like to try your suggestion for a week and then hear their ideas of how to improve the situation.

Even with older children or all-adult households, it's okay to suggest trying out your idea before family members suggest changes.

For example, if you are the only person clearing the table, at the next meal suggest that family members form a line from table to sink and pass the dishes along. With young children, you can sing as you work. With older children you might suggest a contest to see who can guess how long it will take to clear the table. In all-adult households, you might pass the dishes to one end of the table where one person scrapes, another stacks, and the rest carry the dishes to the kitchen.

When it's time to put toys away, instead of falling for the old "if-you-don't-do-it-for-me-I'll-cry-or-scream routine," work with the kids. Sit in the middle of the room, pick up one toy and ask "Where does this go?" while handing the child a toy to put away. Work as long as your child does. When the child stops, you stop. Instead of a power struggle, make it a game.

Another way to simplify routines is to schedule deadlines you can monitor. If you aren't present at the deadline, chances are your children will forget to follow through, and so will you.

Creating Deadlines Alleviates Problems

Make sure to create a deadline for every routine. We find using the expression "by when" helps family members understand the meaning of deadline. With school-age children, suggest special times for doing jobs with deadlines you can enforce. For example:

Before breakfast (by when), the children should have their rooms cleaned, clothes on, and beds made. If those tasks aren't done, place their breakfast plates upside down on the table as a nonverbal reminder that they have something to finish before sitting at the table. They can return to the table as soon as the work is done. Children don't need to suffer to learn, so don't try to rush clearing the table to "teach them a lesson."

Before dinner (by when), have a ten-minute family straightening time. Gather all the family members together, set the timer and pick up all those personal belongings, dirty dishes, etc., that have been left lying around the house. You probably spend at least ten minutes a day complaining about the messes, so remind yourself that, even though this may be inconvenient, it's a better use of your time to work with your family than to pit them against you.

Spend time once a week with each child in his or her room helping them sort through the chaos. Suggest the child do this before playing with friends or watching television. Be present to help your child get started if the job is overwhelming.

Working together with a deadline helps older family members, too. Ask if someone would like company or help going through piles of collected messes. Suggest you work together before lunch on Saturday (by when) or before a Sunday outing (by when). Offer to help family members sort through their clothing to see what fits and what doesn't before the next shopping trip. Help pack out-of-date items for storage or charity before returning seasonal items to the closet.

With your leadership, your family can create rituals and structure that soon become part of the way things are done in your home. As family members become more proficient, they can accomplish more frequent and difficult tasks.

Adding Routines and Creating Family Traditions

Perhaps family members started out helping by emptying the dishwasher before dinner. Later, they added a job after dinner, such as clearing the table. Next they might add chores before breakfast, such as cleaning their rooms and making their lunches for school, or they can help one day a week with major housecleaning or yard work.

There are many opportunities in any household for family members to participate. Consider some of the following for your home:

During Saturday morning shopping, ask the children to help you by finding a can of fruit or a box of cereal. You might give younger children pictures or labels on cards that they can match up. With two or three cards, they have their own shopping list. If they can read, suggest they find the cheapest can or the one with the least salt or fat. Show them how to read labels so they can succeed. Not only will they help the family, but they'll learn about nutrition and develop intelligent consumer habits.

Before bedtime on Sunday, water the plants. Give each person a watering container and a section of the yard or house to water. Do it together and the work will get done in no time.

On laundry day, ask for help folding towels or carrying clean clothes to the children's rooms. If the children are old enough, give them baskets of their own, put the unfolded laundry in the baskets, put the baskets in their rooms, and let them decide where to put the clean clothes. Older children can pick a laundry day and, with your help, learn to run the washer and dryer so they can do their own clothes.

Make young children their own cleaning kits: feather duster, small broom, and so on (for outdoors it might be a small shovel and a short rake) so they can work with you. Thank them for what they do. Don't complain when they leave before the job is done.

Cook with your children. Try something simple to take on a picnic. Make something more time-consuming and let it sim-

mer while you play a game. Let the younger children peel vegetables or spin the salad spinner. Older children can read the recipe aloud while you gather the ingredients from the pantry. Teach children to use blenders and beaters to whip up a smoothie. Use large bowls to avoid overflow and provide children with special cooking aprons or hats. Remember to have fun.[1]

On special occasions—for example, when company is coming—instead of sending the kids outside to get out of your hair, let them contribute to the event by finding jobs they can do. Perhaps they can make personalized place cards, put candy and nuts in bowls, make table decorations, or arrange hors d'oeuvres on a plate.

Working together as a family can be great entertainment. One family of four created such a fun-filled event on shopping day that their friends asked to come along and help. The ritual started on Sunday afternoons when they planned the week's dinner menus. Everyone in the family suggested dinner ideas, which Dad wrote on a large erasable calendar. Mom made a grocery list and read it off to family members who sat at the table with paper and pencil, writing down the items they wished to collect at the store. Before they left home, someone set a stopwatch to see if they could complete the shopping in an hour.

Everyone piled into the car and headed to the store, where each grabbed a cart and took off in a different direction. About twenty minutes later, they met at the checkout counter, done. Then it was home again, where all helped unload the car, put away the groceries, and fold the bags. Breathlessly, the family ran to the stopwatch to see how well they did.

---

1. Thanks to Laurie, Neil, Noah and Logan Stolmaker for cooking tips from their book in progress, *Kids in the Kitchen: A Recipe for Success.*

Developing routines helps family members learn to think ahead and be more sensitive to what needs to be done. By developing routines, household members will minimize the stresses of living together and learn how to handle responsibility.

Creating Routines Takes the Stress Out of Juggling Work and Home

Many adults wonder how they can juggle home and work or, in some cases, school, home, work, and more! Creating family routines helps with the juggling act. Since you no longer have to be responsible for everything, you can give yourself permission to relax and do things you enjoy. It really is okay to take care of yourself and be good to yourself! Put your feet up, read a book, go for a walk, play tennis, rent a video, talk to a friend, fly a kite—anything you like to do for yourself. Once routines are firmly in place, you and the rest of your family will have more freedom, spontaneity, and harmony.

CHAPTER 5

Increasing Cooperation Through Shared Decision Making and Family Meetings

A young woman watched a mother and her elementary school-age daughter prepare to order from a restaurant menu. The mother asked the child what she wanted and discussed her preferences at length before ordering. The woman watching had been raised in a family where no one ever asked children what they thought. As she relayed her story to one of the authors, she said in amazement, "Can you imagine growing up in a family where people actually talked to each other?"

We can imagine, and we know that children do better when they are listened to and taken seriously. We know that children who learn to think through the consequences of their decisions have better self-esteem. And we know that children who are involved in decision making treat others with more respect, as the following stories illustrate.

Three-year-old Jake got angry when his four-year-old cousin Patti kept knocking down his fort. Several times he asked Patti to stop, but she didn't listen. Finally, Jake grabbed Patti's hand, pulled her toward his little table and said, "Patti, we need to have a meeting."

Jake lives in a family that holds regular family meetings, and at age three, he knows the way to solve problems is to talk

63

about them at a meeting. Many children his age solve problems by hitting, kicking, biting, crying, or tattling to a parent. Jake has already learned better tools for conflict resolution.

Two-year-old Ellie is learning from her parents, Ted and Gita, that her opinions are important. Whenever she says no her parents say, "Let's talk about it a little first." Then they ask Ellie what she wants, say how they feel, and offer Ellie limited choices. Ted and Gita realized Ellie was catching on to negotiation skills one night when Ted said, "Come on Ellie, time for bed." Ellie pursed her lips, looked Ted in the eye, and said, "Talka little."

These families are raising children to think and have opinions. Instead of directing and controlling their children, the parents empower and encourage them by providing opportunities to learn respectful decision making. They focus on building their children's skills gradually rather than coercing them to behave the way they want. The parents see the family situation as filled with opportunities to teach children skills to make their lives work better.

If you want your family members to express feelings and opinions and be involved in solving problems, we recommend you begin developing their skills by practicing the following suggestions. Even though all the examples involve children, the pointers in this chapter work with household members of any age. Use your imagination to create examples that fit your household.

1. **Ask your children what they think at least once a day and listen to their responses.** For instance, ask, "What do you think you could do to help the family get ready for dinner?" If your child answers, "I could make decorations," don't jump in with, "That's not what I meant." Seriously consider what your child says before you respond.

2. **Offer a limited choice whenever possible.** "Would you like to bring the silverware or the plates to the table?" or "Would you like to feed the dog before dinner or after dinner?"

3. **Help young children think about the consequences of their behavior by asking, "If you were the mommy or the daddy, what would you do when your child does this?"** Two young boys volunteered to rake the leaves and stopped after raking only a fraction of the yard. Their father asked, "If you were the dad, what would you do about the job your sons just did?" The boys grinned sheepishly and said, "We'd ask the boys to finish."

4. **As your children get older, spend time each day asking how things are going and listen to what they say.** This is a simple way to become aware of your children's opinions and thought processes. One family asks a question each night at the dinner table, like "What was the most embarrassing moment of your day?" or "What made you the angriest/happiest today?" Everyone in the family takes a turn answering, and all have fun sharing and listening.

5. **Don't ask your children if they would like to do something if the answer "no" is unacceptable.** "Would you be willing to take your little brother with you to the park?" is a request, not a command, so be sure it is acceptable to hear no for an answer. If not, say, "I'd like your help. Please take your little brother to the park so I can get some things done without any interruptions."

Trying these techniques can help you develop a habit of involving your family in decision making. As children practice thinking things through and learn to trust that you really want to hear their ideas, they become more creative and confident. It's time to take involvement another step: allowing and encouraging your children to find solutions to problems with each other without your input. By giving the children a chance to problem-solve without your advice, you can find out what their abilities are, as well as enjoy some simple solutions to complex problems.

Allow Your Children to Work Out Solutions Whenever Possible

If you think your responsibility is to fix everything and that you are the only one with good ideas, notice how creative the children are in the following examples. They came up with inventive solutions to difficult problems with no input from their parents.

The Swanson children were fighting over whose night it was for the dishes. Their mother, Andrea, said, "I'm tired of hearing you argue every night. I'll bet you five dollars you can't figure out a way to solve this problem without fighting."

Her children looked at her in amazement then one asked, "Five dollars apiece, or do we have to share it?"

"I'm so sure you can't figure out a better way that I'm willing to bet five dollars each," Andrea said with a grin.

The children retreated to the living room and were back in less than five minutes to collect their money. "Mom, we figured it out. We divided the dishes into two parts and we'll do the dishes together every night. We'll take turns doing "first part" and "second part."

"Do I need to know what's in the 'first part' and the 'second part?' " asked Andrea.

"Just watch and see how well our idea will work. We figured it out and we're not going to argue about dishes any more. Can we have our five dollars?"

"How about trying your idea out for the rest of the week to make sure it works. Then I'll give you the money." By the end of the week, Andrea Swanson was congratulating herself on the best ten-dollar bet she ever lost.

In another family, the children were fighting over the new popcorn popper. Their father unplugged the unit and said, "When you've worked out a way to use the popper without fighting, you can try again."

At first the children grumbled, but later one said, "We worked it out. John can make the popcorn on Mondays and Wednesdays and I get it on Tuesdays and Thursdays. Friday is free day. We both agreed."

If the children start squabbling again, Dad can simply say, "Try again. The plan seems to be falling apart. Let me know when your plan is worked out so you can use the popper again."

Sometimes children will come up with a totally new plan to get things done. In a family where everyone did the gardening and watering together, one child volunteered to mow the lawn every week if he didn't have to do any other yard work. Everyone in the family was tired of listening to his complaining, so they agreed to try the new plan for a month. When the family sat down to evaluate at the end of the month, everyone had noticed much less grumbling and hassling over yard work and was pleased with the way things worked.

Another group of children helped solve the forgetfulness problem by suggesting that each child have a tag with their job list on one side and their picture on the other. The children agreed to check their tags before dinner. When their jobs were completed, they would turn the tags over to their picture and go to dinner. If their jobs weren't completed, they would do them before going to the table. One parent looked at each tag before dinner to see whether a smiling face or a list of chores stared back. If the parent noticed a list, he or she called to the child, "Come here and show me your smiling face." Everyone knew that was the signal to get to work and complete agreed-upon jobs.

A family of five children solved the laundry room chaos by deciding to each pick a day to do laundry. They all agreed that if a brother or sister forgot the wash in either the washer or dryer, the next person using the laundry room would put the forgotten laundry in a plastic bag and set it outside that sibling's bedroom door. The parents were thrilled with the sugges-

tion, which ended the squabbles among the children and eliminated piles of dirty clothes in the laundry room.

Even though children can solve many problems without
adult interference, they sometimes need adult help. If you are having trouble with reoccurring problems, you can help your children
solve them by listening to their feelings and sharing yours then
working together to come up with a plan you all can live with.

Listen and Share Feelings to Find Win/Win Solutions

Feelings give important information about why problems are
occurring. If your children are angry or resentful, listening to
their feelings can help you and them move beyond a stuck

place. When you listen to your children's feelings, you communicate that feeling the way they feel and thinking the way they think is okay. You are practicing unconditional love and acceptance when you let your children know you hear and understand their feelings without finding fault, explaining away their feelings, or fixing things for them.

Your children may struggle when they first try expressing feelings. They'll use statements that include the words "like, that, as if, you, or they" following the word "feel." These words indicate what they are thinking, but not how they are feeling. For example, "I feel like I can't do anything right" is a thought not a feeling. "I feel discouraged" expresses a feeling about not being able to do anything right.

Help your children express feelings by listening to what they tell you and reflecting back the contents as you fill in these blanks:

"You feel _____ because _____ and you wish _____."

Eight-year-old Marguerite complained to her father that two-year-old Cassie was spoiled and not doing things the way she was supposed to. She objected to the way Cassie set the table, with silverware in the wrong place and the napkin covering the entire place setting. Marguerite said she would get in trouble if she set the table that way, but everyone laughed when Cassie did it.

Instead of arguing or invalidating Marguerite's feelings, her father said, "You're feeling *upset* because *we laugh when Cassie does things wrong and when you make a mistake, you get in trouble,* and you wish *we would correct Cassie, too.*"

Marguerite looked at her father with surprise and said, "No, I don't want Cassie to get in trouble. She's only two. But I wish you would laugh at me the way you do Cassie."

"Oh, honey, are you jealous that Cassie gets a lot of attention?" asked Dad.

"Everyone thinks she's so cute and treats her like a baby. I wish she wasn't so spoiled."

Her father tried again. "You're feeling *hurt* because *Cassie gets away with things and you're expected to act like a grown-up* and you wish *we would stop spoiling Cassie.*"

"Yes," said Marguerite, "how is Cassie ever going to learn to do things the right way? When I was two, I couldn't put the napkin on top of the plate."

"Sweetheart, would you like to hear a story about you when you were two?"

Marguerite was intrigued and said, "Tell me what I did when I was two."

"You had a very special way of setting the table. We made a shelf just for you that you could reach, with all the dishes and silverware on it. At least ten times a day, you used to set the plates on the chairs, put the silverware on the plates, and sit on the floor and pretend you were eating. Then you would call Mommy and me over and tell us to sit on the floor with you. Then you would instruct us to eat everything on our plates. You were such a cutie!"

Marguerite smiled as she heard the story. "Did I really do that? Maybe Cassie will grow up and learn to set the table right when she's my age."

"Yes, honey, I think that will happen just like it did for you. But if Mommy and I are scolding you for making a mistake, you can tell us that your feelings are hurt. I'm sorry if I said something that hurt your feelings."

"It's okay, Daddy," said Marguerite, as she went off to play with her toys.

In another family, Mrs. Talivera argued daily with her six-year-old daughter Amelia about her messy room. When asked to clean her room, Amelia had a tantrum so Mrs. Talivera decided to try listening to her daughter's feelings. She said, "You're feeling angry because it is too hard to clean this mess alone, and you wish I would help you?"

Amelia corrected her and said, "I'm not angry, I'm tired, and I don't want to clean my room right now."

At this point, Mrs. Talivera decided to let Amelia know how she was feeling by using the same formula: "I understand that you are tired and would like to wait till later. Perhaps we could do that, but I have another problem. I feel upset because we are fighting, and I wish we could figure out a way to work this out without fighting."

"Well," said her six-year-old, "you always want me to clean my room when I'm tired."

"You're upset because I pick a bad time for you to clean your room, and you wish I would ask when you aren't tired?" queried Mrs. Talivera.

"Yes, and I don't like it when you yell at me either."

"Would you like to work out a plan so you can do your room when you're not tired and I can stop yelling? That would make me happy, too, because I don't like to fight with you. If we wait too long, your room will get so messy that it will be too hard to clean. I wonder if cleaning your room right before dinner might work better. Are you tired then?"

"No, I'm hungry."

"Maybe I could let you know when it's fifteen minutes before dinner. We could set the timer and you could clean your room then. Right before we sit down to eat, you could come and get me and show me your room. If you need help, I could spend a few minutes before dinner with the parts that are too hard for you. Would you like to try this out today?"

"Okay, Mom, but no yelling," said Amelia, as she gave her mother a big hug.

Amelia's mother practiced a simple problem-solving method with her child. First she listened to her child's feelings. Next she shared how she felt. Finally she made a suggestion and asked if they could try it out for a short time. If Amelia had given a different suggestion, Mrs. Talivera might have started a list of ideas and suggested they pick one to try for a few days. Finding a solution both people can live with, based on information gained by listening to feelings, is an easy way to come up with win/win solutions.

A weekly, regularly scheduled family meeting is a way to put together all the skills in this chapter. A family meeting is a time for family members to solve problems, express feelings, get appreciation, and have fun. Family meetings work with any age group or family configuration. We have talked to people who use this format with great success at their office, in the dormitory or sorority house, as well as at home.[1]

Hold Regular Family Meetings

Family meetings are the most effective tool to improve cooperation in a household. They are excellent for working out shar-

---

1. See *Positive Discipline in the Classroom: How to Effectively Use Class Meetings and Other Positive Discipline Strategies* by Jane Nelsen, Lynn Lott, and H. Stephen Glenn (Rocklin, CA: Prima Publishing, 1993) for detailed information on using this concept in the classroom.

ing chores but can be used to discuss any issue important to family members. Use these meetings to coordinate schedules, plan for rides and attendance at important events, give out allowances, and choose menus for the week. Some families like to end their family meeting with a family fun activity or a special dessert.

Family meetings should be held once a week for everyone living in the house. Make sure there are no other distractions, such as TV or phone calls. Sit around a table or in the living room. If a family member chooses not to be involved, hold the meeting without them and let them know they are welcome to join at any time. Set a time limit for your meeting from fifteen minutes to a half hour. Items not completed can be handled at the next family meeting. During the week, post an agenda, usually on the refrigerator, where everyone can see and write on it. Young children might draw a picture of their problem. As issues come up, instead of trying to solve them in the moment, write them on the weekly meeting agenda. That way, all those who are part of the problem can take part in finding a solution.

Start each meeting with compliments and appreciations so everyone gets an opportunity to say and hear something positive. Depending on the age and skill level of family members, you can take turns leading the meeting and writing down agreements made. After compliments, the chairperson calls off items on the agenda and helps family members take turns practicing respectful communication. This is a good time to practice the problem-solving skills in this chapter including asking family members for their opinions, sharing and listening to feelings, and offering choices.

It is important that everyone in the family agrees before a change is carried out. This agreement is called consensus. Until you reach consensus, you might have to live with things the way they are. Some subjects need to be discussed for several weeks before a family can come to consensus. Brainstorming (generating a list of suggestions without evaluation) creates choices everyone can consider. Instead of seeking a perfect solution, suggest that family members choose one from the list of brainstormed ideas to try for a short time. Set a family meeting to evaluate the solution and discuss what everyone learned by trying it out.

Family meetings work best when everyone focuses on solutions rather than problems and who is to blame for them. No one should be in trouble at a family meeting and everyone should be listened to and taken seriously. We recommend using family meetings to discuss items of interest to the children before jumping in to solve the family chore problems. Once family members have practiced listening to and helping each other, you will have an easier time working out the details for family chores.

Create a Plan for Sharing Chores

If you wish to use a family meeting to create a plan for sharing household chores, try the following suggestions which work for many families:

- Let everyone know you need help.
- Ask what work must be done for the family to function smoothly. Write down all tasks even if they seem silly. Don't worry about missing a few.
- Ask if each person would be willing to pick one to three things to do for one week.
- Decide when and how often each job needs to be done and set a deadline (by when) for finishing it.
- Create and post a chart with the information.
- Have the person previously responsible for each job train the new person.
- Assign one family member to check the chart each day to be sure the job is completed by the deadline. If the job is not done, this person is responsible for telling the volunteer it is time to complete the job. (It is best that the job of reminding be given to a child or to the less involved parent.)

Don't try to get all the jobs assigned at once. Overwhelming everyone with tasks would make winning cooperation difficult. Since this is just for one week, you can make changes and add more jobs later.

Another way to share chores is to ask family members to list jobs that need to be done. Write each job suggested on a small slip of paper, put the paper into a bag, and ask each person to pick one to three jobs for the week.

With young children, you can use the family meeting to choose a time of day everyone can help each other with chores. Then together create a chore wheel that you can rotate each day to assign one job for each family member (see page 56). Plan and work when everyone is present.

If family members think one person should do everything, appeal to their sense of fairness by asking, "Who thinks it's fair for one person to do all the work? Who wants to do all the work? I don't, so I'd like us to work together."

In one family meeting, the family solved the problem of house cleaning by agreeing to clean the house together once a week. Since the mom did most of the cleaning up to that point, she suggested that she list the tasks in each room and teach the rest of the family how to do each part. The family members decided to have each person clean two rooms of the house and work together. Mom agreed to assist until everyone felt competent to do the tasks without her help. The family decided to pay themselves for their work and use the money for family outings. By working together as a family, what used to be drudgery for one became a relatively easy job for many. It took the family less than an hour a week to make the house sparkle.

Another family made a list of chores to put on the kitchen table every morning. During the week, family members completed jobs when they had time and marked them off. Weekly cleaning was finished when all the jobs were marked off.

In another family, Dad wrote all the jobs on slips of paper and put them in a bag. Included on the slips of paper were some items like "Go outside and sing a funny song" or "Rest for five minutes." Each family member did the assigned job he or she pulled out of the bag, including the "fun" things.

Exploring Jobs for Children

Some families aren't sure what jobs are age-appropriate when the children say, "Let me do that!" or "Can I help?" The following list suggests work possibilities that suit different age groups. Think of the list as a start rather than as an all-inclusive selection limiting what children can do.

Tasks for Two- and Three-Year-Olds

Pick up toys and put away   Dust
Sweep the floor   Set the table
Vacuum   Help prepare meals

Scrub vegetables
Stir ingredients
Empty waste basket
Water the lawn
Help clear the table
Help put groceries away

Put salad ingredients in bowl
Shake small rug
Help in garden
Feed pets
Wipe up spills
Scrub the sink and tub

Tasks for Four-Year-Olds

Set the table
Help compile grocery list
Feed pets
Help make beds
Help wash the dishes
Dust
Help cook (make desserts)
Hold mixer
Empty dishwasher

Put groceries away
Find items at grocery store
Help with yard and garden
  work
Vacuum
Load the dishwasher
Make sandwiches
Get cereal and milk
Get the mail

Tasks for Five-Year-Olds

Help with menu planning
Make sandwich and clean up
Add ingredients
Scrub the sink, toilet, and tub
Sort clothing for the wash
Answer telephone
Take garbage out
Water the plants

Help with grocery shopping
Pour beverages
Clean room
Clean mirrors
Fold clean clothes and put
  away
Help clean out the car
Help paint their room

Tasks for Six-Year-Olds

Water plants and flowers
Peel vegetables
 Help hang clothes on clothes
  line

Cook simple foods; tortillas,
  eggs
Prepare own school lunch
Stack wood

Rake leaves   Take pet for a walk
Straighten and clean out drawers

Tasks for Seven- and Eight-Year-Olds

Take phone messages   Sweep and wash patio area
Care for bikes   Wash cat or dog ←
Carry in grocery bags   Do simple ironing
Wash down walls and floors   Fold blankets
Clean up animal messes   Pick berries
Clean refrigerator   Carry in firewood

Tasks for Nine- and Ten-Year-Olds

Mop and buff floors   Clean blinds
Sew buttons   Clean storage room
Read recipes and cook meals   Bake
Cut and arrange flowers in vase Help with barbecue
Help with painting   Polish silver
Pick fruit   Wash car
Buy groceries for school   Do own laundry
   lunches   Clean backyard furniture
Change sheets   Weed in garden

Tasks for Eleven- and Twelve-Year-Olds

Clean stove and oven   Mow the lawn
Clean pool   Barbecue foods
Help build things   Run errands
Chop kindling   Stack firewood
Look out for younger   Iron
   siblings

Use these lists to generate further ideas and ask family
members for additional suggestions. Sometimes, it is the child's
experience rather than age that makes tasks appropriate. Re-

member that work is simply tasks to be done, which can be mastered with desire and training. As tasks become routine, they become easier.

Solve Problems as They Come Up

If someone complains that he or she is doing too much or someone else isn't doing a job properly, put the problem on the agenda to discuss at the family meeting. If you think that family members can do more chores or that it's time to switch jobs, put those items on the agenda. Be willing to change your system if it's not working. Don't lock in to something your family doesn't like even after they've tried it for a while. If something isn't working, wait until the next regularly scheduled family meeting to discuss the problems and brainstorm alternatives. Waiting a week to change might allow time to solve a problem, as family members are capable of learning from mistakes.

The Franklins used a family meeting to solve the fighting over who got to sit in the front seat of the car. Both mother and father were tired of the squabbling. The family brainstormed ideas and chose the suggestion that one person sit in the front seat on the way to the activity, the other person on the way back. Eleven-year-old Matt said he would ride in the front on the way to the destination, and Dora, age nine, said she would ride in the front on the way home. The family agreed to try the idea for a week.

At the end of the first week, Matt put the item back on the agenda. He complained that Dora got to ride in the front seat longer because of the car pool schedule. Most of the trips in his car were on the way home, and he didn't think it was fair that he got stuck in the back seat. Mrs. Franklin said that she was also disappointed in the new plan because there was still a lot of fighting in the car over who sat where. She thought it would be best to have both children sit in the back until the family solved the problem. Matt protested again, saying Dora had a whole week in the front, and now he would get even less time. The meeting ended without a solution, but everyone agreed to continue thinking of options.

At the third week, Dora put the item on the agenda. She and Matt had figured out a solution for sharing the front seat that they would like to try.

"What did you work out?" asked Mr. Franklin.

"I'll sit in the front on odd days and Matt will sit in the front on the even days unless we are going on a vacation. Then we'll count the number of days we'll be away and take turns. If it is an uneven number, one of us will get the front in the morning and the other one in the afternoon. We also decided we get the front seat on our birthday," Dora reported.

"Wow, that sounds complicated. I don't think I can keep that straight," said Mom.

"Don't worry," chimed in Matt, "if we start fighting, just tell us to sit in the back seat for a day and then let us try again. We know the plan. Right, Dora?"

"Yes, and we both agreed," said Dora.

Everyone decided to go with the new plan, which worked without a hitch for years. By using the family meeting to discuss issues, listen to feelings, and reach consensus, most problems can be solved.

Occasionally, family members refuse to cooperate or help with anything. Using the methods in this book should prevent this, but if there is a complete breakdown of respect in your situation, a strike may be necessary.

Use a Strike When All Else Fails

A strike is an extreme measure which should only be used as a last resort, after trying the other suggestions in this book. A strike is based on the premise that you have the right to want others to be involved in household responsibilities. You may not be able to win their cooperation, but you can decide what you will or will not do. A strike is just that. You decide to take care of only your needs—prepare food for yourself, make your bed, clean your clothes, put dirty pots and pans in a soapy bucket, keep a clean pan to use for your meals, and so on—but refuse to take care of the other household members' needs. It's important not to use a strike as a threat or a means of coercion.

If you take this drastic step, be prepared for the disorganization and chaos that will ensue. Let the household members know what you're doing then follow through while maintaining a friendly yet firm attitude. Don't cave in when your fifteen-year-old pleads that she has nothing clean to wear to the dance and her life will be ruined. Reply in a sincere and friendly tone that you're not going to do the wash or lend her your clothes even though you know how hard this must be for her. After experiencing the discomfort of chaos for a few days, most household members are willing to come together and discuss what changes need to take place. When this happens, use the suggestions about beginning to work together in Chapter 2.

One household experienced the effects of a strike for six weeks before cooperation was restored. If you work by agreement and not by assumption, your family is unlikely to come to the point where a strike is needed or would last that long. As we stress throughout this book, people resist helping less when they know they have a choice.

The more you practice shared decision making and family meetings, the more life skills your children will learn and the closer your family will become. By emphasizing working things out instead of finding fault and pointing fingers, everyone will feel less defensive and act more responsibly. If you go through a period where family meetings are less effective, go back to the skills at the beginning of the chapter, practice them, and trust that you will find your way back to harmony and cooperation.

CHAPTER 6

Managing Money and Handling Allowance

Wouldn't it be nice if your children could handle money responsibly and you could help them learn to do so? Parents who lack skills and training in money management often have difficulty deciding how to handle money with their children. Even parents with poor money management skills can overcome their backgrounds and help their children become good money managers by using the suggestions in this chapter. We discuss how to give an allowance, create jobs for pay, deal with credit and loans, and establish a clothing allowance.

What Is an Allowance?

Many of you received money from your parents when you were children. Perhaps your parents gave you money as a reward or a bribe for chores, for "good" behavior, or for doing something that pleased them. Perhaps your parents withheld money as punishment if you didn't do the chores or misbehaved in some other way. Or perhaps you were given money arbitrarily, in varying amounts which depended on your parents' whims. Some of you may have received money for good grades or lost hope of receiving any because of poor grades. Perhaps your family struggled financially just to survive and there was no money for you. It's no wonder if you aren't prepared for the job of training your children to use money responsibly.

Allowance is the tool you can use to teach your children how to make wise decisions and use money responsibly. Learning to handle an allowance is like learning any new skill. Your children will need training and the chance to learn from making small mistakes. We suggest you start this training process by giving your child an allowance when he or she first expresses a need for money. This typically occurs when the child is about three years old and is on a trip to the supermarket.

Mrs. Dixon had her shopping list in hand as she entered the supermarket with her toddler. As she lifted her three-year-old daughter into the shopping cart seat, Susie lunged forward trying to reach the gumball and toy machines close by. "I want candy," Susie cried, expressing her first need for money. Parents might think suggesting that a child this age can understand or handle an allowance is silly. We believe that young children understand far more than adults give them credit for and that they are capable of making decisions about themselves and their world that they carry into adulthood. You have a wonderful opportunity to begin training your children to handle money by allowing them to make small mistakes and learn from those mistakes at this point.

When Mrs. Dixon returned home, she sat on the floor with her daughter and said, "Susie, you wanted something from the machine at the store. I think you're ready for an allowance so you can get something next time we go there. Would you like that?" Susie smiled at her mother. Mrs. Dixon said "Good! Friday will be payday. I'll give you a quarter for the candy machine." Susie started playing with her blocks again.

Friday, Mrs. Dixon gave Susie a quarter and said, "Here is your allowance, Sweetie." Susie took the quarter, looked at it, and put it in her pocket. Two days later Mrs. Dixon found the quarter in Susie's pants pocket when she was doing the laundry.

With a chuckle, she put it in her own pocket and set it aside for next week's allowance. She did not mention it to Susie.

On the next trip to the supermarket, Susie ran to the candy machine and said, "I want one!"

Mrs. Dixon asked, "Have you brought your allowance?"

Susie looked up at her and repeated, "I want one," then started to cry.

Mrs. Dixon calmly replied, "Next time bring your allowance and you can get one." Instead of feeling sorry for Susie or rescuing her, she gently took Susie's hand, walked her over to the cart, and lifted her into the seat.

During the next few months Susie often lost her quarter, but sometimes she remembered to bring it in her little change purse and made her purchase. Gradually she learned that she had to remember her allowance if she wanted to buy something at the store, and she did.

How Much Allowance Do I Give?

The amount of an allowance should be based on your child's age, needs, the resources of your family, and your discretion. Twenty-five cents a week was appropriate for Susie at age three. She couldn't buy much for a penny or a nickel. As a rule of thumb, you might figure on 25 cents for the three-year-old and increase the amount by 25 cents for each year the child has had experience with money. You might raise the allowance to 50 cents a week for an experienced four-year-old, then to 75 cents a week for your five-year-old. When this formula stops working, it is time to renegotiate. The best place to do this is at the family meeting (see Chapter 5).

Helping Your Children Learn to Budget

To help older children learn to figure out how much money they need and how to live within their means, you can introduce the idea of a budget. This works well with school-age children, beginning in elementary school and continuing through college. When your child learns to budget money during the school years, he or she is building skills to carry into adulthood.

A good way to begin helping your child learn to budget is to ask, "What are your expenses?" Many children respond by saying, "I don't know." If this happens, ask your children what items they want you to buy for them during the week, and say, "Let's make a list." Be sure to include the items and the amount needed for each item for a week. You might remind them of purchases you remember them asking for. The goal is to start your children thinking ahead about what they want and calculating the costs.

Children don't have to think about what they buy when someone else pays. When they are out shopping and see something they want, they simply ask you to buy it. Whether you buy it or not often depends more on your whims than on your budget. Your child doesn't have to put that purchase in a context of whether he or she has the money for it or not. We have often heard a child ask for something and the parent respond: "I don't have enough money." The child replies, "Write a check," or "Get some more at the bank." Such patterns of irresponsible or unconscious spending developed in childhood often continue in adulthood.

The parents of a seven-year-old, a twelve-year-old, and a sixteen-year-old decided to give the kids an allowance. They said, "We have been paying for things you ask for during the week. Sometimes you want something and we say no. Sometimes we feel irritated that you are asking for money. We realize that you need money and would like to help you learn more about money by having some of your own each week. We would like to start you with an allowance, and we need to know what you think you will need each week." The children responded with the items listed below.

Sample Budgets

Seven-year-old		*Twelve-year-old*		*Sixteen-year-old*	
Gum	$ .60	Movie	$2.00	Movie	$ 5.00
Book	$2.00	Gum	$ .60	Gas	$ 7.00
		Snacks	$2.00	Snacks	$10.00
		Hot		Makeup	$ 3.00
		lunches	$3.00		
	$2.60		$7.60		$25.00

Once you have listed the items and the amounts, you have identified the child's needs. Next, consider what might be appropriate for children of that age, what things really cost, what is necessary, and what the family resources are. The amount of experience the child has handling money is also a factor.

Once you have agreed on an amount for the allowance, give your child his or her money and set up a deadline to reevaluate the amount. We suggest waiting at least a week but no more than a month to reevaluate. In the meantime, leave it up to your child to decide how to spend his or her money. Your child will soon learn that if she wants to go to a movie but spends the money on comics, there won't be enough for the movie. Decide ahead of time how much money you are willing to give up control over so your children can learn from their mistakes. Starting out a sixteen-year old with $25 a week may be more than you can comfortably give up control of and more than she needs to gain experience in handling money. Or, if your child wants to spend $10 a week on snacks, you may be unwilling to let him spend that much money in that way.

The parents in the example felt the seven-year-old's request for $2.60 was reasonable, so they agreed on that amount. The twelve-year-old's budget was a little high, so the parents said they felt $6 a week was more appropriate. They suggested the child might save some of the allowance each week and go to a movie once a month, or chip in with a sibling or friends to rent a movie. They reminded their young teen that they had extra jobs for pay (see more information on jobs for pay in this chapter) to help him make up the deficit.

The sixteen-year-old's budget exceeded the parents' estimate by $10 a week. The parents explained their own budget limits to her and said they would be happy to do some problem solving to help her figure out how she could make things work. Instead of denying her needs, the parents were willing to help her take the responsibility to find a solution. When she agreed to their help, they again mentioned the movie rental idea or going to the movies less often. They offered to take her to the local discount food store to buy inexpensive snacks. They suggested she ask her friends to chip in a dollar for gas to help cover the cost of picking them up and taking them to school.

The teenage daughter asked if she could earn extra money when she babysat for her seven-year-old sister. Her parents considered this request and said they would be willing to pay her on weekends, but not during the week. She thanked them for being willing to help her earn extra money. The family agreed to try out the new allowance plan for a month and evaluate it at a family meeting.

Once the amount of the allowance is agreed upon, it should be given on a regularly scheduled day and time. After some discussion the above family decided Friday at 6:30 would be payday. Parents are responsible for remembering to provide the allowance at the agreed-upon time and for being consistent and reliable.

As your children get used to handling money, introduce the idea of a savings account or other money management tools. A sixteen-year-old might enjoy opening a checking account and learning to use an ATM card. When you see your children handling money responsibly, you may want to add more money to their allowance for them to manage. It's up to you, but many children are responsible enough to pay for weekly lessons, tutoring, dues, etc., out of their allowance. The idea is to gradually transfer more and more responsibility to your children.

Supplements to an Allowance— Jobs for Pay

Perhaps you've noticed we haven't suggested paying family members to do regular household work. We believe that work teaches children responsibility, skills, cooperation, and the importance of being a contributing member of the family. Household jobs which need to be done so the household can function should be kept separate from allowances. The danger in paying kids for doing jobs is that they may learn to do work only when they get something for it. Will they pick up their socks only when they get five cents a sock? Being a member of a family means sharing responsibility for work to be done. We believe, however, that children should receive allowance because they're part of the family and are entitled to a share of the family's "wealth," as well as an opportunity to learn to use money responsibly.

We do suggest paying the children for jobs that we would hire someone else to do. For instance, one father was taking his car to the local car wash, spending $8 each time. When his kids asked for ways to make extra money, he told them he'd be happy to hire them to do the job for the same amount of money.

We recommend keeping a list of jobs for pay along with the amount to be paid for each job on a bulletin board or on the refrigerator so anyone who wants to earn extra money can do so. We suggest discussing standards and working out how payment will be made before the job is confirmed and paying for the work "after" the job is done. This can prevent the problems of unfinished or sloppy work.

```
 ⌐ JOBS FOR PAY ⌐

Washing      = $1.00 per
  Windows            window
               (inside & out)
Cleaning
  Counters   = 50¢ per
                   counter
Giving Buddy = $3.00
  a Bath
Washing the Car = $5.00

Stacking Wood = 5.00 an
                     hour
```

Gloria, age ten, and her brother Dirk, age eight, were home on a Saturday afternoon. Gloria decided she wanted to buy a new book. She looked in her wallet and realized she was short about three dollars. Payday was tomorrow, and her parents didn't make advances. She remembered the list of "Jobs For Pay" that her family compiled. She went to the refrigerator and saw that her parents would pay $8 to have the family car washed. When she asked her Mother to back the car into the driveway so she could wash it, Dirk heard her and chimed in, "I want to wash the car too." Gloria thought for a moment and replied, "Okay, you can help me and we can each get $4."

Mother backed the car into the driveway while Gloria and Dirk got the bucket, hose, soap, rags, and sponges ready. They hosed the car and started washing it. After about a half an hour, Dirk put his sponge down and went into the house to find his Mother. "I want my $4. I'm finished. I don't want to do any more." Mother replied, "I pay when the job is done. You'll have to work it out with your sister." Dirk went off to play in the backyard.

An hour later Gloria came to Mother and announced that she was finished and wanted to be paid. She asked if Mother would take her to the bookstore. When Mother went to get her purse, Dirk came in for his half of the money.

Gloria said, "That's not fair. You didn't finish the job, Dirk. You left and went to play while I washed the car. You shouldn't get anything."

Dirk protested, "I did too wash the car, but I got tired."

"Well I don't think half the money is fair. You didn't do half the work," Gloria cried.

Mother returned with the money and said, "Dirk did some of the work, but he didn't finish. What would feel fair to you, Gloria?"

"Well, he shouldn't get half. How about if I get $6 and Dirk gets $2?"

"I want more. I washed the tires and they're hard to do. That's why I got tired," cried Dirk.

"How will you work this out?" Mother asked.

"How about $3 for Dirk and $5 for me," Gloria responded. That was something they all could agree on. Mother distributed the money then took Gloria to get her book.

Should We Interfere with Our Children's Spending?

It is essential that your children have freedom of choice in their spending. You may worry that they will make a spending mistake. You might think an item is overpriced or of poor quality. Motivated by your fear of mistakes, you tell your child it is not okay to buy the item in question. You give your rationale, but your child probably won't see it the same way. In fact, he or she may feel thwarted and think you are unfair. After all, whose allowance is it? In the effort to protect your child, you rob him or her of an opportunity to learn through experiencing the consequences of behavior (a wonderful teacher for us all), create resentment, and damage your relationship. Hardly the results you intended!

We recommend the following to influence your children and help them learn good decision making skills.

1. Share your ideas without insisting your child follow them.
2. Support your child by being non-judgmental.
3. Acknowledge your child's feelings.
4. Allow your child to experience the consequences of his or her behavior.
5. Help your child assess what he or she has learned from the experience.

Twelve-year-old Maria and her mother Celeste were shopping for tennis shoes. When Maria found the pair she'd been looking for, Celeste gasped at the $105 price tag. She'd never spend that much for tennis shoes for herself! Secretly she hoped they wouldn't have Maria's size in stock, but the sales clerk returned smiling, with a box of shoes the right size. Maria tried them on and loved them. She looked at her mother who said, "Maria honey, the budget is tight this month and I can't spend this much on tennis shoes. I expected to spend more like $50; $105 is a lot of money for tennis shoes!"

Maria replied, "I know, but everyone has these. I just got money for my birthday. What if you pay the $50 you planned on and I make up the difference with my money? The clerk said I get 10 percent off, which makes them $95. I checked some other stores last week and they were charging $120 to $125 for the same shoes. This is a good price for these, and I really want them."

Celeste refrained from imposing her judgments on her daughter. She listened to her daughter and realized Maria had done some comparison shopping. She was honest about her finances and shared her opinion with Maria instead of imposing it on her. Our experience has been that the more we are honest and share our ideas with our children while letting them experience the consequences of their decisions, the better they get at making wise spending decisions.

Timmy was six and he loved trucks. One day he came home and proudly showed his mother his purchase. He had bought his friend Mark's old truck with his allowance. Mother noticed that the wheels seemed loose and was concerned that Mark had taken advantage of her son, but she didn't say anything. A little while later Timmy came to her crying. "What's wrong?" she asked.

He held up the wheels that had fallen off the truck. "Look what happened," he sniffled. "I'm never buying Mark's toys again!"

"Sounds like you learned something important," his mother replied.

A few days later Timmy told his mother that Mark wanted to sell him another truck and he told Mark he wasn't buying his old toys because they broke. He decided to save his money and buy a new truck.

Timmy's mother allowed him to experience the consequences of purchasing an old item. She also supported her son
by being non-judgmental, validating his feelings and helping
him understand what he could learn from the experience. This
paved the way for future opportunities for Timmy to trust his
judgments.

Should We Give Credit or Loans?

We do not recommend making loans or extending credit to
your children when you begin giving them an allowance.
When you are training children in money management, you
must think carefully about what you want to teach them. If
your goal is to teach them to use money responsibly and you
rescue or bail them out, you may end up defeating your pur-
pose. Hold firm and follow through, even though doing so is
difficult.

Tammy had been giving her son George, age eleven, an
allowance for five years. One Saturday George asked if he could
go to the movies with his friend Tony. Tammy thought about
her plans for the day and replied, "Sure, I can drop you both
off downtown this afternoon. What time is your movie?"
George said he'd look in the paper. He soon returned and told
Tammy the movie started at one o'clock and that he'd need
money.

Tammy said, "You got your allowance for this week."
George explained that there was a great sale on comic books
and he had spent it all. Tammy simply replied, "I don't do
loans and Tuesday is payday." George nodded and walked away
to call his friend. A little while later Tammy noticed Tony had
come over and the boys went out to play. That evening George
told Tammy that he and Tony would go to the movies next
week. Tammy said, "Let me know what time so we can coordinate a ride."

Once good habits of responsible spending are developed, you can loan money to your child when the need arises. For example, your daughter may see a tape she wants at the music store and ask if you'd loan her enough to buy it. She promises to pay you back at home with money from her savings' envelope. You take a risk (small at first) and make the loan. When you get home your daughter dashes into her room and returns with the money she owes you. She's just established herself as a good credit risk.

If, on the other hand, your daughter dashes to her room to play her tape and later that evening you have to remind her she owes you money only to get put off again, she has established herself as a poor risk at this time. Refrain from further loans until this one is resolved and explain why. This affords everyone an opportunity to learn from their mistakes.

Adding More Financial Responsibility: The Clothing Allowance

A clothing allowance is another tool you can use to teach your children lifelong habits of responsible spending. We recommend starting this after your children have had experience with a basic allowance. If you talk about purchases and cost when your children are young, you can start them on a clothing allowance as early as third grade (eight years of age). By then they are ready for another step in handling money. Once again, start the training process with small steps. Eventually you can turn the entire responsibility over to your children and let them handle all their clothing purchases.

How much do you spend on your children's clothing each year? Most parents would answer, "A lot, but I don't really know the exact amount. I buy what they need." Clothing for children can be very expensive, often putting additional strain on the family budget, and shopping for it can be stressful.

As your children get older, they become interested in more than whether their clothing fits. The style and brand name can seem crucial to them. Conflicts often develop over what you believe is important and what your children consider important.

If you haven't been paying attention to what you spend on your children's clothing, we suggest you begin to keep track. This will help with future planning. Look through your checkbook for the past month or collect clothing receipts over the next few months to get an idea. Determine how much money you can or want to make available for your children's clothing in the future. Let your children know this. Establishing clear limits is important in the training process, even though the numbers might not mean much to your children in the beginning.

Children enjoy starting off the school year and heading into summer with new clothes. Incorporate this into your plan by scheduling clothes buying outings in early fall and in the spring.

Mrs. Thomas had been giving her children an allowance for a few years. Her daughter Dawn turned eight in July and was about to start third grade. Mrs. Thomas decided Dawn was ready to learn more about money and spending and spoke to her husband about what she wanted to do. "I think Dawn is ready to learn more about spending. She already does a good job of managing her allowance so I'd like to start her on a clothing allowance. I've been keeping track of what we spend on her clothing. I think $500 would work for this year. She can spend up to $300 next month and $200 in the spring. What do you think?"

"Wow, that sounds like a lot of money," he replied.

"It is, but we actually spent a little more than that this past year without really being aware of it. I think this will help us spend less and help Dawn learn more about making decisions. I'd like to keep her equipment for soccer separate from this. I don't want her to find she's spent all her clothing allowance

and doesn't have money for her uniform. Since it's important to us that she play soccer, I'd like to set it up so she can play without us having to rescue her."

Mr. Thomas said, "Good idea. I think I'll like knowing what we're spending instead of seeing the bills come in. Maybe we can set aside the money in advance."

The next day the Thomases talked to their daughter about her clothing allowance and made a date to go shopping. Mr. Thomas said he'd like to take his wife and daughter for lunch and shop with them to see how this worked. Mrs. Thomas spent the next half hour showing Dawn, by using her paper dolls, how she could make nine different looking outfits out of three tops and three bottoms.[1] Later Mrs. Thomas made arrangements to send their son to the sitter's on shopping day, knowing he wouldn't enjoy the shopping trip for his sister.

---

1. A special thank you to Barbara Mendenhall of Family Education Center, Petaluma, CA, (707) 762-8835, who so graciously shared her new article, "*Anna and the Amazing Allowance*," with us.

The following Saturday, the Thomases went to the mall. Dawn brought her calculator with her. In the first store she picked out an armful of clothes and she and her mother went into the dressing room. Dawn tried on everything, discarded some of the items, and added up what was left. The total came to $250. Dawn asked, "What do you think, Mother? I love this sweater and pants outfit."

"I think they're really nice. You have a great eye for color. Do you think you need five new sweaters?" Dawn thought for a minute and said, "Probably not. What I really need is new pants. The ones from last year are too short. I think I'll get the pants outfit and the blue sweater here and go to another store to look more."

"Why don't you model the pants outfit for Dad and tell him your plan?" suggested Mrs. Thomas.

Dawn put on the outfit one more time and went to show her father. "Honey," he said, "you are a great shopper. How about we break for lunch and then continue?"

After lunch, the Thomases continued the process—considering, modeling, adding, subtracting, comparing, wondering, and deciding. When the family left the mall, Dawn had purchased two sweaters, a jacket, five pairs of pants, socks, underwear, two skirts, a pair of shoes, three pair of boxers, four pairs of tights, a dress, and a pants outfit. She still had $9.50 remaining in her clothing allowance. She was quite satisfied with herself and asked her parents if she could keep the money she had left over in case she thought of something she wanted later.

Mrs. Thomas said, "I'll make a note in my checkbook that you have $9.50 left, and when you need something, we'll shop again." The Thomases knew that at first it was best to keep a tally of Dawn's spending and pay for the clothing rather than give her the cash. As she gained more experience shopping, they might give her the cash or even give her money each month to set aside for clothing. Many children manage a monthly clothing allowance, setting aside money for big purchases and buying clothing as they need it. As you can see, following the suggestions in this chapter helps children acquire many money management skills. By the time your children head for college or move out of the house, you will want the training process to be completed, with them assuming full financial responsibility. We don't mean your children have to be self-supporting, even though many are when they leave home. What we do mean is that, even if your children have their own checking account and credit card, they are responsible for managing and reconciling these accounts. In other words, they make their own spending decisions and are responsible for paying their bills.

Continuing the Allowance Through College

If your children do go on to college, you will find that many colleges send tuition and housing bills directly to the students. Some don't even send bills! Students are often responsible for knowing when payment is due and paying it on time. If it's not made, they can't register for classes—a direct and meaningful consequence for their behavior! You can make deposits into your student's account for tuition and housing costs each semester or quarter, based on a budget both you and your child discuss and agree upon. Deposits for monthly expenses can be handled in the same way. We recommend regular check-ins with your student to make needed adjustments and prevent problems from developing.

Mr. and Mrs. Peters had been paying Jordan's tuition and housing expenses plus supplying a monthly allowance of $200. This agreement worked for a year and a half. Every couple of months his parents would ask how things were working, and he would assure them that things were fine. Then, Jordan told his parents he needed a car to drive to a job site for a special project in one of his classes. Since Mr. and Mrs. Peters did not want to buy a car for Jordan, they suggested he ask his grandparents if he could borrow their extra car for the semester. They were happy to help him out.

A few months after Jordan got the car, he called his dad to say he was having trouble meeting expenses. Jordan found that he was spending more money on gasoline than he had anticipated. Mr. Peters told him he would speak with Jordan's mother and get back to him in a day or so. He thanked his son for calling and assured him they would work this out.

Mr. and Mrs. Peters discussed the problem. Already feeling the pinch of increased college costs in their budget, they decided they could help Jordan out with an increase of $50 a month for the next three months then return to the original $200. They would suggest Jordan look for part-time work to supplement what they were able to provide if he needed more money. They called Jordan that evening to tell him what they were able to come up with.

Jordan was grateful for their help and told them he had already done some checking. He had a possible job lined up for the summer that he hoped might become part-time when he started his next semester. In the meantime, the additional $50 would help pay his bills. Mr. and Mrs. Peters were grateful that years of spending and budgeting practice helped Jordan get to this point.

In contrast is the story of Mr. Lyman and his son, Andrew. When Andrew started college, it was the first time he had any responsibility for managing money. His father gave him a credit card and opened a checking account in Andrew's name at the local branch bank. He told Andrew to keep his expenses down to the basics, and Andrew agreed.

Two months after Andrew started school, his father received a call from the bank saying Andrew was overdrawn by $300. Just a few days before, Mr. Lyman noticed that Andrew was charging restaurant meals and expensive clothes on his credit card. Furious, he called Andrew to tell him he was overspending and that, if he couldn't be more responsible, he would take away the credit card. Andrew begged his father for another chance. He said that things cost much more than he realized but it was important for him to keep up with his fraternity brothers so he wouldn't get a reputation of being "cheap."

Mr. Lyman was still angry, but he didn't want his son to be unpopular with his fraternity brothers, so he said, "Okay, Andrew, I'll pay these bills and cover the overdraft this one time, but don't let it happen again."

"Thanks a lot, Dad. You sure are a great father. I'm glad you understand how tough it is when you're just starting out. I know I learned a lot from this so I'm sure I'll be more careful."

We won't go on with this story, because we're sure you can guess what happens from here.

Helping Children Who Don't Go to College

What happens if your children don't go to college and are finished with school? Financial help at this point may vary from nothing at all to covering all costs. That decision is based on the family's budget and your child's circumstances. If your child is helping himself, you may want to supplement him financially while he makes the transition from home to independent living. Some parents refuse to help children financially unless they go on to college; but for some young people, college right after high school, or ever, is not a good choice.

We recommend handling support in a respectful way: sit down with your child and find out what his or her plans are. Be extremely clear about how you intend to help. You might offer free rent at your house while your son or daughter gets established in a job or training program. If you are unable to give financial support, you can lend emotional support and ideas, knowing you have valuable lessons to offer.

Many young people feel overwhelmed with the responsibilities after leaving home and are often afraid they won't be able to find a job. They often take advantage of parents who don't set clear and reasonable deadlines.

When Jack finished high school he told his family he would attend summer school at the Junior College to take "How to Study" classes before signing up for college in the fall. He thought he could handle a part-time job along with his coursework. The plan sounded good, but Jack slept until noon each day and made no attempt to find a job. He missed the deadline to register for summer school, so the coursework never materialized.

Jack said he didn't realize how sick of school he was, and that a summer vacation was just what he needed to be fresh for school in the fall. His parents said, "Jack, we can see that making the transition from high school to college or the real world is difficult for you. We're willing to help you by providing room and board as long as you are helping yourself. You have until October to get it together. That should give you ample time to find a job, get registered at the Junior College, and decide whether taking courses is for you. If you don't want to go to college, we will support your decision, but you can't continue to live here unless you are making progress in taking responsibility for yourself."

Jack said, "That's more than fair. Don't worry, I'll handle it."

When the end of October came, Jack was still unemployed and had decided he didn't want to go to college. It was clear to his parents what help he needed, and they knew it was going to be painful for everyone. They knew Jack was a capable, wonderful person who was scared and confused about how to take the next step. He resisted their attempts to help or give advice, and they respected his right to learn from his experiences. With this in mind, they told Jack it was time to move out. They said they loved him enough to provide him with a growth opportunity. Jack said he understood, packed his bags, and moved in with his friend's family.

It took another six months for Jack to get serious and realize that he didn't want to spend his life sleeping on his friend's bedroom floor and sneaking into his parents' house for showers when they were at work. His parents maintained contact and invited Jack for dinner once a week, which he graciously refused. Jack was angry, but he used his anger to get his life working. He found a job and a house to share. Each step he took to get his life working gave him confidence and pride. A year later, Jack came for dinner and thanked his parents for their faith in him and their help. He said that a lot of his friends were still living with their parents, not working, and not going to school. He knew he would have been in the same place without the "encouragement" from his family.

The earlier you begin helping your children learn money management skills, the easier it is for them when they move

away from home. Jack had little responsibility handling money before he left home, so he had some hard lessons to learn without the opportunity to learn gradually and make small mistakes along the way. By starting your children with an allowance, creating jobs for pay, and teaching them to manage a clothing allowance, you give them the skills that make transition into adulthood easier.

CHAPTER 7

Maintaining Cooperation with Teens

It seems curious that a person who looks like an adult could act like a young child, unless that person is a teenager. It's particularly difficult to get cooperation from teens (sometimes known as workers from another planet). Helping the family is seldom high on a teen's list of priorities. In fact, family chores may not be on the list at all. You may even wonder if your adolescent is still part of the household, as he or she spends more and more time away from home and is often too preoccupied to count on even when home. Of course, you are still concerned about getting help with the family chores, which haven't diminished just because the child living with you has transformed into an adolescent. And the more you want help, the less help you seem to get. If you get angry and try to motivate your teen while under the influence of anger, you invite power struggles and rebellion instead of cooperation. You and your teen get better at fighting rather than accomplishing anything constructive around the house.

Your teenager is at that difficult time between childhood and adulthood. How your child's behavior is affected by his or her individual maturation process is more of an indicator of adolescence than chronological age. If you aren't sure whether

you are dealing with an adolescent, ask yourself the following questions:

Is your child more concerned with friends and self than with family?

Does your child seem selfish, self-centered, and irresponsible?

Is your child alternately very sweet and very moody?

Would your child rather talk on the phone, listen to music, or stay in his or her room than be with the rest of the family?

Does your child complain about your nagging when you think you are making simple requests?

Does your child suddenly get inspired to do the work of ten, only to revert to a state of lethargy for days on end?

If you can answer yes to any of these questions, chances are you are dealing with a teenager. In that case, much of what used to work in the past will now be ineffective. There is hope for cooperation, but you'll need to change your methods. We recommend the following:

1. Make room for differences.
2. Use your sense of humor.
3. Be sensitive to the needs of the "untrained worker."
4. Be creative and change what isn't working.
5. Practice joint problem solving, create mutually agreed upon deadlines (by when), and follow through.
6. Loosen the reins and encourage more adult responsibilities, including work outside the home and caring for a vehicle.
7. Tap into teenage humanitarianism.

Make Room for Differences

Are you a person who cleans the kitchen as you cook or a person who leaves the mess until later? You probably have your own style for accomplishing things. If you expect your teen to do things your way, you invite unnecessary power struggles, since your teen is in the process of defining how he or she is different from you. Since the obvious way to be different is to do the opposite, insisting that things be done your way is asking for trouble.

Your teen sees the world through a very different filter than you do. If you think your teen is trying to make your life difficult and take his or her behavior personally, think back to when you were that age to get in touch with how a teen thinks and feels.[1] Instead of making assumptions about your teen's motives, talk about and agree on standards before starting a job to prevent problems from developing later. Keep in mind that your teen is

---

1. For more information on parenting teens, consult *Positive Discipline for Teenagers* (formerly titled *I'm On Your Side*) by Jane Nelsen and Lynn Lott (Rocklin, CA: Prima Publishing, 1994).

sensitive to your tone of voice and facial expression. A sharp or sarcastic tone with an angry scowl won't invite cooperation.

If you think your teen is intentionally doing poor work, instead of criticizing, ask your teen whether the job meets his or her standards. If your teen feels satisfied with the work, allow yourself to consider a different standard of cleanliness. If you think your teen is taking advantage of you, say: "Try again, I think you can do better" or "The job isn't done. Please finish it."

One of the most volatile issues with teens is the condition of their rooms. Even the neatest child lives in chaos at some point during the teen years. Make allowances for your differences and don't make rooms an issue. Allow your children to decorate and set the standard of cleanliness for their rooms so they have a bit of the universe to control. If the room offends you, ask your teen to keep the door closed or close it yourself when you walk by. You might make an agreement with your teen that chaos is fine during the week, if once a week the room gets vacuumed and dusted, the bedding is changed, and the dirty dishes are returned to the kitchen. When you stop fighting over rooms, teens are more likely to cooperate with work in other parts of the house.

Be flexible when your teen has friends over and doesn't get things done according to the regular schedule. Unless it is a genuine inconvenience to you or other family members, relax and trust your teen to do what needs to be done once their friends leave.

Teens think you are nagging when you talk about problems that might happen, such as telling a teen he *might* forget to do his chores if he doesn't do them at the agreed-upon time. A teen is more apt to work with you if he or she can see that there really is a problem and if you say what your issues are. A fifteen-year-old boy was informed that he consistently forgot his chores when his friends were over and didn't do them later on his own. He asked his mother why that was a problem, and she said, "I can't concentrate or work in a mess, so I have to wait for you or do your job for you before I can get started with my work."

Her son looked at his mother as if she came from another planet and said, "I didn't know you felt that way. How about this? If I don't do my work before my friends arrive, I'll ask them to help or listen to music in my room until I'm finished?"

His mother thanked him for his consideration of her feelings and said, "That would work just fine."

When her son left the room, she called her friend to get a reality check. "Missy," she said, "Am I losing my mind? I could swear I've talked to Ralph at least a hundred times about forgetting to finish his work when his friends are over, and all he does is get defensive. This time I explained why it was a problem for me, and he initiated a solution without any prodding. What happened?"

Missy couldn't stop laughing. "Sue, don't you know that teens don't like to do things because you say so, but they love to help you out with *your* problems? I think you've lost your sense of humor with Ralph and are taking him too seriously. You think everything he does is meant to get you, but I don't think you're really all that important in his life right now. Don't get me wrong. He loves you, but his head is elsewhere. Remember when you were that age? Were you really thinking about your parents twenty-four hours a day? Get a grip!"

"Thanks for the dose of reality, Missy. You're right, I am too serious." Using a sense of humor is one of the most effective tools for creating cooperation and harmony with a teen. If you've lost your sense of humor like Sue, read on.

Use Your Sense of Humor

Remember when your four-year-old dressed like a super hero to go to the grocery store and your three-year-old insisted on having the crust cut off his sandwiches before he would eat them?

You probably thought your child was adorable. Maybe you even took a picture for your photo album or called a relative to tell stories about how precious your little one was. Now the same child is behaving in age-appropriate ways (for a teenager) and you are considering sending him to live with a distant relative instead of laughing at his uniqueness. What happened to your sense of humor? If you can get it back, you can make the teen years a lot more fun for everyone.

Teenagers enjoy a sense of humor and respond to it much better than to lectures and nagging. The following situations illustrate how parents used humor to invite cooperation and to lighten things up.

When a teenage girl forgot to set the table, her mother served the dinner directly onto the table. Everyone laughed at the absurdity of the situation. The table was set on time from then on.

In another family, Mom lost her sense of humor during menu planning because she thought the family members weren't taking things seriously. One of her teens imitated her trying to save money by planning meals from available ingredients. Her son looked over the staples in the cupboard and said, "Now we have a lot of popcorn, paper towels, and rice left, so Dad, why don't you make a rice, popcorn, and paper towel casserole tonight?" Mom laughed along with everyone.

Peter Conklin, a father of three teens, used betting and guessing games to motivate his children and add humor to a situation. When Peter noticed the chores weren't getting done as agreed, he'd say, "Someone forgot to do something they agreed to. I'll give a dollar to the first person who guesses what it is." The teens ran around the house trying to find what hadn't been done so they could win the dollar. Another time Peter said, "I'll bet two dollars you can't finish your yard work before the football game starts." His bets and games were effective because they were used infrequently and unexpectedly. Had Peter used bets as rewards and bribes, he would have inferred the only reason his teens helped the family was for the money, and they would have felt less respected.

One day at the grocery store, in the same spirit of fun, Peter tore the shopping list in half and gave one part to his son and the other to his friend. "I'll take you two for pizza if you can find everything on your half of the list in fifteen minutes. Go!" Shoppers watched in surprise as the two teens ran through the store tossing items in their carts.

Sometimes a sense of humor is the only way to get things done. When Sharon Anderson's fifteen-year-old stepson Cole moved in with the family, it wasn't long before his presence was felt in the household. First her hairbrush disappeared, then half the kitchen towels, and finally several blankets vanished. He paced, twisted, twirled, and danced as he talked on the phone until the cord became a tangle of knots. Cole left his dirty dishes, magazines, and soda cans in Sharon's bedroom, where he lay on her bed to watch TV each day after school because his own room was too messy. The final straw came when Sharon started to set the table and couldn't find any silverware in the drawer, and the kitchen scissors she used to cut up some spices was missing.

"Cole Peter Anderson," Sharon yelled, "come here this minute!"

Cole sauntered in and asked, "What are you so uptight about? Did you have a bad day at work?"

Sharon clenched her fists, ready to read Cole the riot act, when she decided to try another approach. She knew Cole was defiant and masterful at defeating adults who told him what to do or who got angry when he didn't do what they wanted.

Sharon paused for a moment then asked, "Cole, have you read your horoscope today?"

"What are you talking about? You know I don't read the horoscopes."

"Well listen to this," Sharon opened the morning paper and, with a serious face, began reading, "Aries: Today is the day you will feel an irresistible urge to return Sharon's scissors to the kitchen, bring all the dirty dishes and silverware back to be washed, untangle the phone cord so it reaches the table, and put Sharon's hairbrush back in her bathroom."

"You're kidding me, Sharon. Let me see that!" Cole grabbed for the paper.

"You run and take care of those things, and I'll cut it out for you to read later," Sharon teased.

Cole grinned from ear to ear and said, "Sharon, you're weird." A few minutes later he brought a laundry basket filled with dirty dishes into the kitchen, replaced the scissors, and started working on the phone cord.

Sharon gave Cole a big hug and said, "Thanks, guy!"

On another occasion Sharon asked Cole if he would like help with his procrastination.

"Sharon, it's a family trait. All the guys in our family do it. It's in our blood."

"Well, I have an idea about how you could change it if you want to, but I'm not going to tell you unless you beg me."

"Okay, Sharon, I'm begging. Please, please, please, what's your idea?" Cole joked.

"Do you know that most actions have a beginning, middle, and an end? I notice that you are good at beginnings, fair with middles, and lousy with ends. Either you get a business card that says 'Cole Anderson, Procrastinator, No Job Too Small to Put Off,' or you try my ABC Happiness Plan."

Cole asked, "What's an ABC Happiness Plan?"

"I can't tell you, but I can show you. Are you ready?" asked Sharon.

Cole knew he was being tricked once again, but Sharon had a way of helping him save face and making things fun, so he decided to go along with her. "Okay, Sharon, I'm ready."

"We'll start with 'A.' Go to your car and bring in all the towels and blankets that belong in the house."

Cole went to his car and returned with his arms loaded. "What next, Sharon?"

"Here comes 'B.' Take all the towels and blankets in your arms and put them in the washer, add soap, and start the machine. Then stand in front of the machine and see if you can guess what 'C' will be."

"I suppose 'C' is that I'm supposed to fold the stuff and put it away," mused Cole.

"Clever boy. I knew you'd catch on to the ABC Happiness Plan. Aren't you feeling happy? I know I am," laughed Sharon.

Cole just shook his head and gave Sharon that special look that said adults can be pretty strange.

Sharon could have turned any of these situations into a confrontation had she insisted that Cole was lazy or defiant.

She decided that she wanted to live in harmony rather than in a war zone. The more she relied on her humor, the more Cole pitched in without a battle.

Sometimes when teens refuse to work, it is for a very different reason than the laziness or defiance parents often assume. If you waited until your child became an adolescent to involve him or her in household chores, your child may not know how to do the jobs and be unwilling to ask for help. Teenagers' defiance can be a cover for embarrassment.

Be Sensitive to the Needs of The Untrained Worker

In many cases, when teens can't do something, it's not because they're inept, but because they're untrained. It's difficult for adolescents to admit they don't know how to do something. Teens like to appear as if they know everything and adults know little.

If you've forgotten that it takes time and practice to learn a new skill, you may expect your teen to catch on automatically, especially when he or she looks so grown up. Learning how to do the job and finding time for training and practice is critical for teens. You need to let your teens know it's all right to not know something and that it's okay to ask for help. You can encourage your teens by focusing on their effort instead of complaining about things that are done sloppily or forgotten. Notice how the mother in the following story avoided all criticism as she helped her sons become involved in family chores.

Paul, fourteen, and his brother Todd, sixteen, hadn't been expected to do much around the house. Their mother, Joyce, did the majority of the housework. She tried frequently to get the boys involved, but gave up after numerous hassles and confrontations.

Her friend asked her to attend a book study group for parents of teens. After a few weeks of class Joyce realized she'd never really taught the boys how to do the chores. She'd just assumed that, as they got older, they knew how to do the work but just didn't care. Now she was ready to try again.

The next day she said to the boys, "I can't do everything around here. You two don't do anything to help."

Paul said, "I have practice after school and homework every day."

Todd said, "I have my job after school. I don't have time to do things around here."

Joyce responded, "I know you both have lots to do. We're all busy, but it's important to me that we learn to work together. I've made a list of the jobs that I'd like help with."

Joyce presented the boys with a list of twenty jobs. She asked each boy to pick one job. Paul said, "I'll scrub the tub," and Todd said, "I'll do the grocery shopping. If I can use the car Thursday, I can go to the store after work." Joyce thanked the boys for their willingness to help and told them that she wanted to set a time to meet and talk about both jobs.

Joyce showed Paul the new scrubber she bought for him to use. They talked about what cleaning product would work, how long the job might take, and what it would look like when completed. Paul even practiced on one spot. Joyce asked, "What do you think?" Paul replied, "It's looks pretty good." They set a time for the job to be done. She talked to Todd about the shopping list, what store he planned to go to, how much money he'd need and the car schedule for Thursday.

Todd came home Thursday with the groceries. While putting them away, Joyce noticed that he'd forgotten two items on the list. Instead of pointing out his mistakes, Joyce said, "Thanks for doing the shopping. I feel so relieved. Your help makes a big difference." "Thanks, Mom," Todd replied as he picked up a few cans and put them in the cabinet. Joyce added the two items to next week's shopping list.

The next afternoon she heard Paul scrubbing away in the bathroom. A little later she heard the front door close and he was gone. She checked the tub and saw cleanser sprinkled everywhere and soapy residue in the tub. When Paul returned, Joyce asked him to go into the bathroom with her. She looked at the tub and asked, "What do you think?"

"It's not so bad. I was in a hurry because my friends were waiting for me."

"Does this look like what we talked about the other day?"

Paul looked down and said, "I guess not."

"Try again. I know you can finish the job," Joyce said as she walked out of the bathroom.

Later Joyce peeked into the bathroom. Paul had cleaned and rinsed the tub, but he left the scrubber on the floor. She walked down the hall and knocked on Paul's door. "I just wanted to say thanks. Your help is really appreciated. Good night." By focusing on progress, Joyce was teaching her sons they could succeed when they helped the family.

Be Creative and Change What Isn't Working

Sometimes your teens are uncooperative because they are ready to make a change. If you notice resistance or procrastination for jobs that used to be done without any trouble, sit down with the family and talk about what's going on. Ask if it's time to change jobs. Are the teens resistant because someone has been nagging them? Is it time for a break from schedules? Do family members need to swap jobs? By the time your children are teens, they may have been doing the same jobs for years. Perhaps they picked the jobs when they were much younger and are tired of them or would prefer doing something else.

In one family the teenage daughter had been clearing the table for nine years. Since no one else in the family was complaining about their jobs, she thought she was stuck. Her mother noticed she had to call her daughter four or five times to clear the table, so asked if there was a problem. Her daughter said she was tired of clearing the table after all these years. Her mother suggested she bring this up at the family meeting so everyone could talk about redistributing the jobs.

"But what if no one else wants to change?" the girl asked.

"Your problems are as important as the other family members'. A family should help one another," said Mother, "We can work this out."

Often routines that worked when children were younger become disrupted by teenagers' work and social obligations. When a thirteen-year-old boy made the cheerleading squad at school, his new schedule interfered with the normal routine. Since practices were held daily from 5:00 P.M. to 6:30 P.M., he could no longer set the table or make the salad for the family's 6:00 P.M. dinner. At a family meeting, he decided he could take out the trash and empty the dishwasher for his sister if she could do his chores until the end of cheerleading season. Adjusting to schedule changes instead of automatically picking up the slack for a busy teen is easiest when your family holds regular family meetings.

When sixteen-year-old Mandy made the volleyball team, she explained that she wouldn't have time to do her chores if she was going to keep up her grades and be on the team. After several weeks of practice, her family was exhausted and irritated by her lack of participation. Her laundry sat in the washing machine for days monopolizing the laundry room and acquiring that pungent odor of mildew. However, she found plenty of time to talk on the phone with her boyfriend. Her brother David resented doing her chores while she sat with the phone glued to her ear.

Dad asked that the family sit down and talk about a problem that came up. At the meeting, David complained about Mandy's lack of cooperation. When Mandy insisted she didn't have time to help the family, her father Dennis said, "Mandy, it's unacceptable for you to not help. We are willing to help you find a way to contribute that fits into your schedule, but all of us are busy and have other commitments too, and we're tired of doing your share."

"I have an idea," said David. "You don't have practice or games on Wednesday. If you can't get your work done during the rest of the week, maybe you could do it all Wednesday afternoon before dinner. I bet your boyfriend would even help if you asked him."

"I'm not asking my boyfriend to do chores for our family. He has enough to do at his place. And how am I supposed to do everything in one afternoon?" Mandy complained.

"That's not our problem," said Dennis. "You have all week, and I think David has an excellent idea. I'd like to try it out for the next two weeks. Unless you can think of a better plan, we'll hold dinner on Wednesday until you complete your work."

"I don't think that's fair, but I suppose I don't have a choice," grumbled Mandy.

The first week, Mandy's chores did not get done. On Wednesday, her father went to her room when he got home from work. "Mandy, it's my night to make dinner. Why don't you let me know when you are almost done with your chores so I can start cooking. I'm making spaghetti, and that takes about a half hour."

"I can't believe you're going to stick with that ridiculous idea of David's," said Mandy. "It will take me till midnight to finish everything!"

Dennis said, "I'll put out some snacks for everyone. We'll wait until you're done to have dinner."

Mandy reluctantly started working and completed all her chores within two hours. The family sat down to dinner at nine. Dennis set the table with candles and had the stereo playing. Not a word was said about the late time or Mandy's attitude. The following week Mandy had her work done by seven. At the family meeting, she said the new plan would work just fine during volleyball season. Everyone breathed a sigh of relief.

A willingness to be creative instead of insisting on doing things the same way turned many potential power struggles into workable solutions for everyone. Another way to win cooperation with teens is to work with them to solve problems instead of telling them what they have to do.

Practice Joint Problem Solving, Create Mutually Agreed-Upon Deadlines, And Follow Through

Conner was a helpful boy who was very involved in family responsibilities. When he turned thirteen and started junior high school, he informed his mother he would no longer clean his room each day or eat breakfast with the family. He thought these things were childish and he was too old to continue the activities he did as a child. Besides, school started earlier, and he didn't want to get up "before the birds" to eat some "stupid breakfast."

Conner's mother Ginny did what most parents of adolescents do: she argued, nagged, threatened, and yelled. Nothing improved the situation. After several months, she realized that Conner was older and ready for a change. She decided to talk with him when she wasn't angry to see if they could work out a solution they were both comfortable with. Ginny knew nothing could be accomplished by arguing at the time the problem was occurring and that she and Conner needed to agree on a time to talk. She approached Conner with a request to talk together, and they agreed to meet when he got home from school that afternoon.

"Conner," Ginny began, "I'm tired of fighting with you every morning; I realize I haven't been treating you respectfully. Do you think we could come up with a routine we could both live with? When you don't have breakfast with us, I miss spending time with you. We hardly ever see each other anymore. I also understand that you don't want to clean your room every day, but I'm not comfortable with the room never getting cleaned."

Conner said, "You don't realize that I'm getting older and you still treat me like I'm a little kid. I'm too tired in the morning to get up earlier to have breakfast, and I want to spend time with my friends after school."

"Do you think it would be too much to clean your room once a week?" asked Ginny.

"Of course not. I could do it as part of the cleaning we do on Sunday," Conner suggested.

"That's okay with me as long as you make arrangements to do it later in the day if you spend the night at a friend's."

"No problem, Mom," said Conner. "If you would drive me to school in the morning so I don't have to ride my bike, we could spend time together in the car. I hate riding my bike to school."

"Conner, I could drive you on Mondays, Thursdays, and Fridays, but how would you get home if you don't have your bike?"

Conner said, "That's easy, I could get a ride home with my friends."

"I feel better about us working this out together," said Ginny, "but I'm still concerned about one thing. If you forget to clean your room on Sunday, I would like a plan so that it gets done without me having to remind or nag you."

"If I forget, you could tell me during dinner, and then I'll do it before I watch TV," suggested Conner.

"Wouldn't that be inconvenient for you?" Ginny asked.

"Sure, so maybe that will help me remember better."

Ginny and Conner both felt better. They had a win/win plan with a deadline they both could live with and a system for dealing with forgetfulness. When a teen is part of the problem-solving process, he or she will either do what was agreed without reminders or respond positively to a parent who says, "What was our agreement?"

Loosen the Reins and Encourage
More Adult Responsibilities

Sometimes adults underestimate what teenagers can do and overestimate what parents should do. As your teens get older, let them take over more responsibility, such as doing all the laundry or the grocery shopping. Once your teen has a driver's license, let him or her do the carpooling or errands that involve the car to get more driving practice. You can teach your teen how to change the oil or do the tune-ups, or keep a service record and take the car to the garage when maintenance is required.

Many teens enjoy working outside the home at jobs such as babysitting, housesitting, washing cars, doing yard work, handling paper routes, doing housecleaning, working as computer consultants, working in local stores or restaurants, tutoring younger children, or hiring out for cleanup projects or construction jobs. We suggest you encourage your teen to work part time and continue their allowance without reducing the amount just because they are earning money. Talk with your teen about the extra costs they can cover with their additional money, or encourage them to save for bigger purchases like cars, college, deposits on apartments, etc.

In one family, the parents were able to hire their son to do filing and typing at their office. The boy felt important and capable and was also able to provide extra income to cover some of his personal expenses. The family took this opportunity to sit down, reevaluate their plan for household work, and make adjustments in his responsibilities.

Even though your teen may be able to handle more responsibility, he or she may make a mistake by taking on too much. If your teens take on more than they can handle, you can help them improve an out-of-control situation without rescuing them. Phil's family had an opportunity to do this when seventeen-year-old Phil purchased his first car. Phil decided he could save money by buying an old car and restoring it. He told his parents he would do the body and engine work with his friends. His mother was concerned because people didn't work on cars in the neighborhood.

Phil said, "No problem, I'll work on the car in the garage."

"But Phil," said his mother, "that's where I park my car."

Phil's father said, "He can use my side of the garage and I'll park on the street until he's done. How long do you think it will take to fix your car up, son?"

"With all the help my friends will give me, I should have the car done in a month," said Phil, deep in magical thinking. Phil's mother wasn't thrilled with the idea, but she agreed to give it a try.

Soon Phil had his tools and car parts spread everywhere in the garage, and neither parent could park inside. His friends soon lost enthusiasm for the project and so did Phil when he

found out how long it took to hand-sand a car. The harder the job got, the less time Phil spent working on the car. And since the car was up on blocks, it couldn't be moved.

Mom could see Phil was in over his head so insisted on discussing the car situation at a family meeting. Mom and Dad discovered that not only was Phil overwhelmed, but the car he was restoring was an embarrassment because nobody in Phil's school drove that type of car. Getting the real issue on the table helped the family devise a plan to get rid of the car. Dad helped Phil put the wheels back on; Mom helped Phil write an ad for the paper; and Phil put the rest of the parts back together. Everyone was relieved when someone bought the car and towed it away.

That left Phil a teenager without a car. Now it was time to help him to figure out how to take on the responsibility of procuring and maintaining an appropriate vehicle. There are many ways to handle this issue. The options range from parents paying for the car and all the expenses to the teen buying the car and paying all the expenses. Whatever the decision, it should be handled in a respectful manner.

Phil's family sat down together and looked at the costs involved in purchasing and owning a car. It was clear that Phil would need financial assistance. His parents agreed to buy him an inexpensive car if Phil paid for insurance, maintenance, and repairs. Phil agreed and found a part-time job to pay for his expenses. The agreement was that Phil could drive the car if the insurance was up to date and the car was safely maintained. If he got behind in any of his payments, he would place the car keys on the table and not drive the car until he caught up.

After a couple of months, Phil quit his job because he didn't like working and instead, sold one possession after another to pay for the upkeep on his car. When he ran out of things to sell, he told his parents, "Owning a car is too much responsibility. I'd like to sell it and ride my bike."

Instead of rescuing him Phil's parents wisely agreed. "We'll do our best to share our cars with you. When you are ready to try owning a car again, let us know. We'll put the money we make selling your car in a special account, and you can use that to help purchase your next car. If you would like a nicer car, you can add to the account until you're ready to take the money out for a car." Phil liked that idea and was relieved to have more time for his friends and school. Phil was part of the decision-making process all along, and he thought the agreements were fair.

What was meant to be a solution to the car problem in the Rivera family, developed into a bigger problem. They began connecting school grades to the use of the car, a popular method many of their friends used to motivate success in school.

Lucy and Manny Rivera had three children, Maria, eighteen, Carlo, sixteen, and Phillipe, eleven. Maria did well in school, but Carlo's grades were poor. His parents knew how important it was for Carlo to drive, so they came up with a rule that he had to get Bs in order to use the car. They told Carlo, "Get Bs or no keys," thinking this would motivate him to improve his grades. The Riveras also pointed out that they were able to save money on their insurance because of Maria's A– average at the Junior College and could get the same discount when Carlo produced a B-average report card.

Carlo promised that he'd work on his grades. In the meantime, he volunteered to do any errand that involved driving so he could use the car more. He began picking up his younger brother, going to the store, putting gas in the car, and picking up his sister from work. Most of his friends were still fifteen, so Carlo felt pretty important when they asked him for rides.

Manny asked Carlo how he was doing in school several times, and each time Carlo assured him things were just fine. When the time came for his quarter progress report, Lucy asked to see it, but Carlo "forgot" it at school. When Manny and Lucy received Carlo's final grade report and saw his C– average, they were stunned.

When Carlo returned from picking up Phillipe at soccer practice, his father met him at the door. Manny held up the report card and yelled, "This is what you think are fine grades! They're terrible! You're not driving the car until you pull them up."

"You don't care about me," Carlo yelled back as he ran out of the house, slamming the door. Lucy listened to this and realized it was going to be difficult to take over the errands Carlo had been doing. She wasn't happy with the way things had turned out.

Carlo didn't use the car for the next week. Then one afternoon he told his mother he had a report due and asked if he could use the car just to go to the library. Since it was school-related, Lucy relented. "Just to go to the library. What time will you be home? I have to pick Phillipe up at practice,"

"I don't know. I should be done by 5:30. I can pick Phillipe up."

Lucy thought for a moment then said, "I guess that's okay."

On the way to the library, Carlo waved at two friends who then motioned him to stop. When they found out he was going to the library, they asked for a ride downtown. Carlo said "Sure" and dropped his friends off at the mall.

When Carlo got home with his brother, his mother glared at him, "You were supposed to go to the library, not go driving around with your friends."

Carlo looked shocked, "What? I did go to the library. I just dropped my friends off at the mall. It was no big deal."

"Well, your father saw you downtown and he's furious. You weren't supposed to be driving anyway."

People in the Rivera household were feeling confused, angry, and hurt. Teens are seldom motivated to improve their grades by threats that they'll lose an unrelated privilege. Not allowing Carlo to drive was actually counterproductive in that it robbed him of the opportunity to cooperate and contribute in his family by running errands.

If the Riveras wanted to relate Carlo's grades to his using the car in a respectful and logical way, they might have had Carlo check the rates at their insurance company. He would have discovered the difference between the regular rates and the good student discount rates. The Riveras could let Carlo know they'd be willing to pay the amount for the good student rate. If it turned out that he didn't qualify, he could make up the difference. That way it would be up to him and respectful to all.

When a teen doesn't see the logic of a plan or thinks an adult is controlling, unreasonable, or unfair, the potential for rebellion—either outward or inward—increases. When teens rebel with passive (inward) power, they appear to be doing what you want, but are actually doing what they want instead. Teens may use excuses like "I forgot" or "I lost it" or "I ran out of time" to defy you. When teens decide to do things and the work is meaningful to them, they are capable of great effort.

Tap into Teenage Humanitarianism

Teens are very altruistic and concerned about the greater good. Help your teens understand that keeping agreements is a trust issue, and that their behavior impacts others. Knowing they make a difference in the family helps teens act respectfully. Let your teen know that you do not wish to take advantage of him or her, nor do you want to be taken advantage of. By helping your teen understand that being part of a family means respecting each other and not taking relationships for granted, you can motivate your teen to care more about other's needs.

Young people can make great accomplishments when they feel what they are doing is meaningful. Twins Shiloh and Sabrina illustrate this. At age sixteen, the twins disliked routine family chores, but they were more than happy to work together on projects that had longlasting benefits for the family. One summer they painted the outside of the house. The next year they put in a sprinkler system and planted a garden. When the family wanted to remodel a room but found the cost too great, Shiloh and Sabrina volunteered to do the labor on the project. Their uncle got them started and supervised the work, but the twins did most of the project. The family was thrilled with the new room, taking everyone who came to visit for a look. Visitors were amazed at the professional job done by two eighteen-year-olds and complimented Shiloh and Sabrina profusely. The twins laughed and said, "We'd rather paint ten houses than do dishes every night. Our folks are willing to pick up the slack during the week because they know we can be counted on for the big jobs!"

If you treat your teens with respect and allow for the changes in their behavior that come with adolescence, you can enjoy them more as well as get a lot more done.

CHAPTER 8

Involving Men in Household Work: Creating Allies Rather Than Adversaries

One of the most common questions we're asked is, "How do you get men involved in helping with household work?" The women asking this question are frustrated and angry because their husbands refuse to help. The husbands justify their behavior by saying, "I earn the money so it's your job to handle the house." Yet even when these women work outside the home, their husbands still think it is the wife's job to deal with the housework.

Women married to men who resist doing household work find it easier to maintain a traditional division of labor than to insist on change. They often feel guilty when they push too hard, because on some level, even THEY think all the work in the house is *their* job. Many grew up in a traditional family and watched TV shows like "Leave it to Beaver," which depict Mom in heels and pearls, hair perfectly coiffed, cheerfully cooking dinner when Dad comes home from work.

Husbands who grew up with the same model picture the family sitting at the table while Mom serves and cleans up, then the children going off to quietly do their homework while Dad sits in his easy chair reading the paper or watching TV. Men and women alike grew up unaware that these pictures would negatively affect their future relationships.

129

Women who continue the behaviors of their mothers or TV models think men have it too easy and start to build resentment. Interestingly enough, that's not what men think. Men we interviewed who came from pretty traditional backgrounds were satisfied with the division of labor in their families. It wasn't until their wives said they weren't happy with things that the men gave any thought to the situation. The husbands were shocked to hear that their wives felt resentful and angry at an injustice in the family that the men hadn't even noticed. As long as their wives handled the house while they went off to their jobs, the men thought everything was fine.

Changing Traditional Pictures Can Be Difficult

Some men, like Jose Ortiz, felt misunderstood and unappreciated when their wives began asking for help. After twelve years of marriage, Jose's wife Donna expressed her resentment concerning the division of labor in their household.

When they started their family, Donna decided to quit her job as an office manager so she could stay at home and care for their children. While Donna looked after six-year-old Raymond and three-year-old Alicia, Jose worked as an accountant in a nearby city. Jose awoke at 5:00 A.M., commuted an hour and a half in rush hour traffic, then spent a frustrating day with clients. He ended his day catching up on paper work at the office then commuted another hour plus to return home. When he walked through the door around eight, exhausted, his children demanded his attention. After roughhousing with them, Jose changed his clothes and sat down to dinner, wondering where the evening had gone. It was after nine by the time dinner was over, and he had to get up at five the next morning. He looked forward to stealing a few minutes alone in his den, reading the newspaper or preparing for the next day while Donna cleaned up and put the children to bed.

One day Donna blew up. "I can't take this any more. I do all the laundry, all the shopping, all the cooking, all the cleaning. My day is as long as yours, and I never get a break."

Jose stared in shock as his wife shouted from the doorway of his den.

Then he responded. "That's your job. Don't I do everything to provide for this family? Don't I mow the lawn every Saturday and wash the car on Sunday? Do you mean to say you want me to do more? Enough is enough!"

Is Jose being resistant and difficult, or is Donna out of line in wanting help? One thing is certain: the family is experiencing a crisis. A crisis can be viewed in two very different ways. The Chinese have captured both meanings in the two characters that represent the word crisis: one means danger and the other means opportunity. Depending on how Jose and Donna or couples like them deal with the crisis, the outcome can be stalemate, divorce, or a renewed, healthier relationship.

Winning Men's Involvement and Cooperation

If Donna backs down when Jose gets angry, she might turn the crisis into danger instead of opportunity. If she makes changes with the children and leaves Jose out, she could sabotage cooperation. As the children become more helpful, Jose could become more resistant if he believes the family is trying to force him into changing.

In situations where a husband refuses to participate, working with the children to win cooperation becomes the only alternative. We think wives can avoid that by following these eight guidelines for involving reluctant partners. Implementing these ideas can turn danger into opportunity.

Eight Guidelines for Involving Reluctant Partners

1. Tell your partner you'd like to work together as a team.
2. Let your partner know there's a problem.
3. Ask your partner for help.
4. Develop a plan by asking what your partner will do and be clear about what you'll do.
5. Set up a time to reevaluate your plan within the week.
6. Follow through with your part of the plan.
7. Reevaluate with your partner at the set time; renegotiate or plan to continue.
8. Share appreciations.

Donna heard about these guidelines at her support group. Donna told her group about blowing up at Jose and said she wasn't sure she wanted to stay with him. She was angry about the imbalance of work and furious that he told her he supported his family financially and shouldn't be expected to do more. She didn't know how to respond to his view. She told the group she couldn't handle everything anymore and was afraid she was headed for a nervous breakdown.

The group facilitator said, "Donna, I don't think you're having a nervous breakdown. It sounds more like you are feeling angry, overwhelmed, and discouraged." Donna was surprised to hear that. It was exactly how she felt. After some discussion, Donna realized her anger was appropriate. She hadn't "signed-up" for the seven-day-a-week, twenty-four-hour-a-day job she now had. She was beginning to understand why she was feeling resentful. It didn't matter that her mother had handled it all; this was too much for her.

After more discussion, she also realized her family was missing the opportunity to learn skills, to cooperate, and to make decisions and problem-solve together. She also realized that everyone would have less to do if family members helped each other. The group suggested she try to win cooperation by

following the "Eight Guidelines for Involving Reluctant Partners." Donna agreed and, with the group's help, practiced what
she would say to Jose that evening.

When Jose came home from work, Donna told him she
wanted them to talk and asked Jose what time would work for
him. They agreed on nine o'clock. After dinner, Donna cleaned
up and got the kids ready for bed. Then she walked into the
den at nine and said she was ready to talk. Jose put his papers
away and joined her in the living room.

Donna began, "Jose, I really appreciate everything you do
and how hard you work. I want us to be partners and work together to bring up our kids." (Guideline 1)

Jose said, "But you're really good at it. You read all those
books."

Donna continued, "It's true I do, but you have good
ideas, too, and I want to work with you. I've come to realize
it's too big a job for me to handle alone. (Guideline 2) I really
need your help." (Guideline 3)

Jose was angry. "You want me to do more. I already work
more than 10 hours a day! I'm exhausted when I get home.
You're home all day."

Donna replied, "We both work hard and the way we're
doing things isn't working for me. We need to get together
with the kids and come up with a plan that can work for all of
us."

"What do you want me to do?" Jose asked.

"I'd like us both to meet with the kids and talk about how
we can work this out. How about meeting Sunday afternoon?"

Jose looked surprised, "You mean during football?"

"What time is the game over?" Donna asked.

"About four o'clock."

"Then let's plan to meet at five o'clock. I'll get a casserole
started early and let the kids know about our plan. We can have
our meeting around the kitchen table. And Jose, thanks for
working on this with me."

Jose reluctantly agreed to the meeting that weekend. (Guideline 4)

On Sunday at five, the family sat at the table. Donna started. "Dad and I talked earlier this week and we want to ask for your help. There's a lot to do to keep this family running." At Donna's suggestion they brainstormed a list of all the work that needed to be done. The list was a page and a half long and included things like cleaning, cooking, and mowing the lawn to making appointments and driving the car pool.

Donna asked, "Wow, who does all this?"

Raymond replied, "You do Mom."

Donna said, "It's too much for one person and it isn't fair. I'd like you to pitch in. I'd like to start by asking everyone to help with the cooking."

"Dad's gonna cook?" Raymond blurted out. "He's a guy!"

Donna said, "Men can cook, and Dad and I agreed that we would like everyone to be involved."

Jose rolled his eyes, "I don't know about cooking; I have a heavy schedule this week."

Three-year-old Alicia said, "I don't know how to cook."

Donna explained that she was willing to teach everyone some basics and go over a few simple recipes with them. When she asked the family to pick a time to help out in the coming week, all she heard was a big "I don't know."

Donna knew she couldn't force the members of her family to cooperate, but she had decided what she was willing to do. She told them, "I'm willing to cook dinner tonight, Monday, Wednesday, and Friday. Alicia and I can work together tomorrow night so she can learn how to cook." Alicia looked pleased, but Jose asked what would happen on the other nights. Donna shrugged and said, "I don't know." Donna suggested the family meet again the following Sunday to continue discussing how the new plan was working. Even though Donna only got one volunteer she decided it was a start. (Guideline 5)

On Monday, Donna and Alicia took a long French bread and sliced it down the middle. Alicia placed sandwich meats, cheese, lettuce, and tomato slices all along the bread. Then they both tore lettuce in pieces and put it in a large salad bowl. Donna sliced carrots, cucumber, radishes, and celery, which Alicia put on top of the lettuce. Donna placed the sandwich and the salad on the table and announced that Alicia's dinner was ready. Three-year-old Alicia beamed, "I cooked dinner!" (Guideline 6) The family sat down at the table and sliced the sandwich where they wanted.

Tuesday evening looked different. When Jose got home a little after seven, Donna was reading a magazine and Alicia was eating Rice Krispies from the box. Raymond ran up to his father and whined, "I'm hungry!"

Jose looked at Donna in disbelief and said, "What's going on? What's for dinner?"

Donna calmly replied, "I don't know; I cook tomorrow," following through on her plan.

Jose grumbled, "I can't believe this! This isn't working" then reluctantly, since no one had signed up for that night, went into the kitchen and made peanut butter and jelly sandwiches for himself and the children.

Donna heard the clattering and banging and decided to stay out of the kitchen until they were finished. Later she made herself a turkey sandwich and cleaned up the plates and jelly knife. "One thing at a time," she told herself. (Guideline 6)

Thursday looked pretty much the same. Jose approached Donna and said, "This isn't working. We have to talk." Donna reminded Jose of their meeting scheduled for Sunday.

Winning Cooperation Takes Time and Patience

This time when the family sat down to meet, Jose began. "We can't go on like this."

Raymond jumped in, "Yeah, I don't like having peanut butter for lunch and dinner."

Jose said, "I don't want to cook dinner. And I can't believe it's okay with you that Alicia eats Rice Krispies for dinner."

Alicia said, "I like Rice Krispies!"

Donna smiled then replied, "I'm glad we can talk about this. I know we can work it out, but I'm not willing to go backwards. I'm willing to cook dinner four nights a week and you agreed to help me with the rest." (Guideline 7)

Alicia said, "I like cooking when you help."

Donna told her, "I'm certainly willing to help you until you can do it by yourself."

"Help me, too," said Raymond.

"Okay, I'll help you both learn to cook until you can do it by yourself."

Jose looked at them and said, "I work late."

Donna said, "Maybe you could pick up something on your way home or leave work a little earlier on your night to cook. Then we'd be covered for every night of the week."

Jose agreed, "Okay, but don't expect anything fancy. I don't cook."

The family divided up the nights of the week. Jose wanted Fridays, Donna agreed to help Alicia on Thursdays and Raymond on Sundays, and said she would cook on the other nights. If she and Jose went out on Saturday, she would prepare something for the kids. Donna suggested that they meet again the following Sunday to check in and see how things were working. (Guideline 7) She shared appreciations with everyone and told them she was glad they were willing to work together. (Guideline 8) The kids seemed excited, but Jose didn't look pleased.

The next week went more smoothly. Jose picked up pizza on Friday and the kids were thrilled. Donna had told her group he might do that and said she thought Jose was copping out instead of learning to cook. The group members suggested Donna focus on the fact that Jose was contributing and needed freedom to do it his way. When the family met on Sunday, everyone agreed things were better and they would continue the new cooking arrangement. As the children's skills developed, Raymond was soon able to prepare his dinners without much help from Donna, and three-year-old Alicia did more parts of the preparation on her own. The family continued their weekly meeting, reviewing the list of jobs they had developed and adding more responsibilities for the family members.

Jose continued to bring home food or cook hot dogs on his night, mostly because he feared he'd lose his marriage and family if he didn't change. He insisted that hot dogs were all he could cook. Since Donna was getting help, she decided not to make this an issue.

After about a year, Jose's attitude changed from grudging acceptance and minimal cooperation to true acceptance and appreciation for the changes. Jose discovered a cookbook of easy-to-follow recipes and expanded his repertoire. Jose became more of an ally in the process as they negotiated and divided the jobs. Donna remained appreciative throughout.

Dealing with Problems That Result from Lack of Skill

One day, Donna asked Jose if he knew why he had been so resistant to changing. Jose reminded Donna that, in addition to his mother and father dividing work in a traditional way, he had grown up with four sisters. His mother organized the girls to handle all the household chores so Jose was exempt from them. When Donna started asking for help, he was convinced that he couldn't do things like cook or work the washing machine. He was secretly terrified that he'd botch the meal, break the washer, or ruin the clothes. Rather than admit that, he claimed he was just too busy to get involved. When Jose mentioned the times he pitched in to help with the children and Donna criticized him, he decided she was better at these things so he'd let her handle them.

It's very difficult if not impossible to do a job when you lack the training and skills required for it. Lack of training in household chores isn't unique to men. Many women experienced disorganization and chaos in their families when they were growing up. As adults, they flounder when it comes to organizing the family or doing anything in a systematic way. When they become partners with men who grew up doing household tasks, they often experience problems, especially if they believe it is the woman's job to manage the household work.

Ken and Rose struggled because of this. Ken grew up in a family of seven boys and one girl. His father died when he was small, and his mother was practical and well organized. She told everyone what they were to do and when to do it. The children grew up expecting to be involved and had plenty of opportunity to learn the skills that come from participating in household work. The boys each had their night to do the dishes, a day to do their laundry, a day to do the dusting and the vacuuming, a night to do the cooking, and a weekly assignment in the yard. They took turns and no one complained. Ken developed many skills and came into marriage expecting to do his share. He didn't think of housework as women's work, but he did expect his wife to organize everything and give assignments to the rest of the family like his mother did.

Rose was the only child of an alcoholic father and a co-dependent mother. Her family life was characterized by loud outbursts, tension, and chaos. Her father was out drinking most evenings and her mother worried herself sick most of the time, complaining and crying in her bedroom. She never seemed able to keep up with things around the house. When Rose's father came home from the bar, he would yell and berate her mother saying, "You're home all day. What do you do around here? This place always looks like a pig sty." Her mother would cry and her father would slam the door to the spare bedroom. As she watched, Rose told herself she would be more responsible than her mother when she grew up and had a family of her own.

Rose and Ken married and had three daughters within a short time. Rose found herself overwhelmed most of the time. She got things started, but it seemed like there was always an interruption, and she was never able to finish. There were piles of laundry in the living room, she was forever late picking the children up at day care, and she never seemed to make it to the store before she ran out of Ken's favorite lunch meat.

Ken was frustrated too. Why couldn't Rose organize things the way his mother did? His mother had had more children and no husband and ran everything smoothly. What was wrong with Rose?

One day when Ken discovered there was no lunch meat for his sandwich, he yelled, "What do you expect me to have for lunch?"

Rose replied angrily, "You expect me to do everything around here."

Ken was shocked, "No I don't, but you never tell me what you want me to do."

Rose yelled, "You have eyes! All you ever do is tell me I haven't done enough or haven't done it right." Rose found herself crying and decided that if this wasn't how she wanted her marriage to be, she and Ken needed help.

Rose loved Ken but recognized that things weren't working. She asked Ken if they could see a counselor together to figure out what was wrong and get some help. After attending a few sessions, they realized they both thought it was the woman's job to run the family, but they had different expectations of how she would run the household. Ken was waiting for Rose to tell him what to do like his mother used to. When she didn't, he found himself criticizing her and thinking that she wasn't doing her job.

Rose lived in fear of being yelled at like her mother and because she had never learned to organize things, she was set up to be criticized by Ken. She was doing her best, which was considerably more than her mother had done, but still had to play catch up most of the time. Rose was hurt by Ken's criticism and lack of involvement. She didn't want to ask him to help out because she was afraid of stirring up his anger.

After several counseling sessions, it was clear that they wanted to work together as a team and involve their daughters as well. Rose knew she could learn to be more organized and to ask for Ken's help. Ken wanted to do his share and realized he had some good ideas to contribute to coming up with a plan for working together.

They started holding family meetings to discuss issues and solve problems together. Approaching one issue at a time made it easier for Rose to ask for help. At the weekly family meeting, the family created a plan they could follow for a week, which solved Ken's need to know what was expected of him and the other family members. He enjoyed the fact that the family was working together. Everyone saw results. The girls gained confidence as their skills increased, and there was less tension in the house.

An interesting turn of events happened one week when Ken and Rose invited two couples over for dinner and a game of Trivial Pursuit. A few days before the event, Rose had a family emergency and had to travel home to spend a couple days with her ailing parents. She suggested canceling the plans with their friends. Ken was supportive of her trip, but he didn't see why they had to cancel their plans for the weekend. Ken saw this problem as a great opportunity for the girls and him to do something special for Rose. Ken met with the girls and offered to make dinner if the girls would do the cleaning. They agreed to help, but said they had soccer Saturday afternoon and needed rides. Ken said he'd be happy to take them to their games if they didn't mind him not watching the games so he could come home and cook. Before Rose left, Ken asked her to make a list of ingredients he'd need for dinner so he could do the shopping, too.

When Rose got home from her parents', the house was clean, the table set, and dinner smelled wonderful. She showered and changed in time to greet the guests at the door. During dinner one of the guests complimented her on the wonderful dinner. "You should tell Ken," she said. "He made the dinner and cleaned the house with the girls' help. I'd been staying with my parents for a few days and just got home a few hours ago."

Rose and Ken's friends couldn't believe Ken had done all this. Ken sat at the table smiling, amused by their reaction. Later that evening when everyone left, Rose told Ken how wonderful everything was and how much she appreciated him. Ken thanked her and told her how much he enjoyed being able to impress their friends. He saw his own pride as another benefit of the effort he and Rose put in to bring cooperation and harmony to their family.

Exploring the Benefits of Men's Involvement

Besides being able to impress their friends with newly developed skills, there are other benefits for men who are involved in household work. We interviewed a number of men who made the shift with their families from a traditional household to one where everyone became involved in household chores. For some of these men, their wife's request for change was a wake-up call that gave them an opportunity to rethink their priorities. Several spoke of creating a better balance between work and personal life that allowed more time for their families and themselves. Others realized the improvements at home carried over to the work site when they began to delegate more and introduce group problem-solving practices to their colleagues.

The men we interviewed were committed to making their relationships work. In their opinion, if their partner wasn't happy, the relationship wasn't working. When they listened to their partner's feelings, they realized how out of balance things had become and recognized that their involvement would benefit their relationship. One man said that it dawned on him that his wife didn't even get a day off, and he wouldn't like working seven days straight. He admitted he might "get a little crabby after a while."

Another man noticed a major shift in his attitude. At first he got involved as a way of "helping out" his wife. After several years he noticed his attitude had changed to thinking, "We're in this together." He mentioned that he and his wife focus on doing what needs to be done based on who has the time and who can get it done. "I have a great sense of satisfaction being able to handle what comes up and staying on top of things so the house looks a certain way. I also have a sense of belonging. This life-style happens because of my involvement. There's a joy about it. And I notice that I don't feel threatened anymore if we are both capable. I used to think I had to be the most capable one in the household."

Another man shared, "We focus on cooperating, not on what's fair. I hardly ever cook. My wife loves to cook—not because she's the woman, but because it's her way of being creative. But if she's busy, I'll cook. It makes sense because it helps us."

Some men saw being involved as an opportunity to get to know their children better and have their children get to know them. They were able to teach the children skills, share ideas and feelings, and spend more time with them by sharing in the driving or being involved in the daily routines. The men were pleased with how responsible their children were and felt relieved to watch the kids go off to college or on to other interests, confident and able to handle their own lives.

They also were happy their children were growing up with a different picture of men and women than the ones they grew up with. When they have courage to change, families can create an environment where members have a sense of belonging and importance and where work is viewed as "our job" because it's "our house." The focus is on cooperation and appreciation for each other.

"Imagine how different it will be for our children, growing up with an attitude of teamwork," said one of our interviewees. "Since we've changed things around here, we're all happier, our communication has improved, and we're more affectionate with each other."

Such families have created a respectful, give-and-take situation in their homes. You may already have respect and give-and-take in your family, so many of the issues in this chapter are not a problem for you. In other families, respect may never occur. We realize some men will never change their attitudes or behaviors when it comes to helping the family. Sometimes resistance is a result of feeling unappreciated for what they do. Other times, misunderstandings and resentments result when you change how you operate and your partner doesn't initiate his or her own change. If you do talk to your partner first and he refuses to work with you, you can certainly start with the children. It will be harder to make changes, but not impossible.

Nick Jones told his wife Jean that he didn't care how many parenting classes she attended or how many books she read, he wasn't doing any work around the house. Jean's efforts to win cooperation consistently failed. She didn't wish to break up her family, but she was unwilling to allow her children to follow Nick's example. She worked with the kids when Nick wasn't around and used many of the ideas presented in this book. Her children were cooperative, capable, and very involved in the family routines. It didn't occur to the children that anything was wrong in the family, as they did not have a picture of a father doing housework and Jean didn't make an issue of Nick's lack of involvement.

One day, her nine-year-old son Derrick asked out of the blue, "Mom, how come Dad never has to help with anything around the house and we have to do all the work?"

"That's a very good question, Derrick. Why don't you ask your father?"

Seven-year-old Doreen, who was listening to the conversation piped in, "Derrick, Dad's already a grown-up and he's too old to learn new things. Mom is growing us up and teaching us stuff so we won't sit around like Dad when we get older."

Jean walked out of the room so the children wouldn't see the surprise on her face or hear her laughing.

Although you have a right to expect everyone who lives in the house to help with the household work, you may have a husband who refuses to budge like Nick. Ultimately, you must decide what to do if your partner persists in treating you and the rest of the family disrespectfully. In a roommate situation, you could move out or ask your roommate to find another place. In a marriage, you would probably avoid those solutions. A power struggle between you and your mate may be a sign of other problems that could be helped with marriage counseling. We recommend you get outside help if you end up in a stalemate.

We also suggest you read and reread this chapter, or even better, the entire book, to find where you may have missed opportunities to encourage cooperation before you throw in the towel. It is worth the time and effort to bring harmony to your family.

CHAPTER 9

Improving Cooperation in Blended Families and Families Experiencing Divorce or Death of a Spouse

Gregory Jordan, a policeman and an avid athlete most of his life, was the king of locker room humor. On a family camping trip soon after he and his new wife Lisa were married, he played a prank on his twelve-year-old stepson Bernie. Bernie left his underwear on top of his sleeping bag in the tent. Gregory took a scoop of chili out of the cook pot, dumped it in the briefs, and left them in the middle of the campsite.

When Bernie saw his underwear, he ran from the campsite, humiliated. His mother Lisa ran after him while his fifteen-year-old stepsister Dani giggled in the background. When Lisa returned after talking to Bernie, she was furious. "Don't you ever treat my child like that again. I don't care how many times your teammates did that to you. My son doesn't think your pranks are funny, and neither do I. I don't think Bernie will ever recover."

Gregory was fuming. "Lisa, you're too soft. I think your son could be fun to be with, but you coddle him so much that

147

he can't take a joke! And when I ask him to help out, he tells me I have no jurisdiction over him so he doesn't have to do what I say. I'm not willing to carry a helpless person. It's time Bernie shaped up and stopped being a baby."

"My son isn't a baby. Before we moved in with you, Bernie helped a lot. He was used to taking orders from me, but he doesn't want you telling him what to do. Now that you've humiliated him in public, I don't think he'll ever listen to you. I know Dani is used to your commands, but my son isn't going to do as you say."

"Lisa," Dani said, "I like the way my dad whipped me into shape. Before I moved in with him, I was lazy. He makes me do things, but I don't mind. Anyway, when you guys aren't around, Bernie does a lot of things to help out. I think he just doesn't want to help you, but if I ask him to do me a favor, he always says yes."

"I'm glad to hear that, Dani," Lisa replied, "but that doesn't change my feelings about your Dad's relationship with Bernie. Gregory, if something needs to be done, I'll talk to Bernie. I want you to leave my son alone."

Gregory, Lisa, Dani, and Bernie were experiencing problems that often occur in blended families. Even though they share a home, they are tying themselves in knots and creating misunderstandings with rules about who can talk to whom and who is right or wrong.

Common Problems That Crop Up in Families Dealing with the After-Effects of Divorce

If you are a parent dealing with the after-effects of divorce, you may have issues similar to the Jordans'. Whether you are a single parent, newly remarried, or part of a blended family, you may have asked these questions:

What do I do when a child says, "This isn't my family, so I don't have to do chores here"?

How do I deal with my spouse's children if they won't listen to me?

How do I stop my partner from treating my children disrespectfully?

How do I handle the chores when differing visitation schedules means we don't have the same children living in the house at any given time?

How do I motivate a child who isn't expected to do anything at his other parent's house?

As a single parent, how am I supposed to juggle everything—earning a living, going to school, getting things done, and organizing the children, too?

How do I make sure I'm not expecting too much of the children?

How do I deal with the pressure my ex puts on me to follow the same routines she does at her house so the children can experience consistency?

You may have already found ideas in *Chores Without Wars* to help with these issues. In the following pages, we offer further suggestions that specifically deal with changes that follow a divorce or death. Even though these changes bring difficulties, the new family structure can also provide opportunities for creating new traditions and routines.

Counseling Is Sometimes the Best Solution for Getting Unstuck

After the camping trip, things went downhill for the Jordan family. Gregory was on Bernie all the time, despite Lisa's order that he leave her son alone. Lisa was so discouraged that she told Bernie to stop visiting until he agreed to help when Gregory asked. Bernie stopped coming to spend time with his mother and said he didn't care. Dani felt bad because she missed Bernie's visits. Because the Jordans felt stuck and didn't see a way out, they decided to seek counseling to get some help.

After they explained their situation to the counselor, she said, "I see this new family is bringing out issues for everyone. Since the two adults disagree on the way to parent, I suggest you try an entirely different method for making decisions in your new family, the family meeting."

At the suggestion of a family meeting, Gregory exclaimed, "I'd rather put an ice pick through my eye than attend a meeting."

"My, that's pretty extreme," replied the counselor, "but if you continue as you are now, I predict that Lisa, in her desperation to please you at the expense of her son, will become more resentful, Dani will turn into the family slave, Bernie will continue to get more angry and withdrawn, and you, Gregory, will become a tyrant. I don't think any of you wants that to happen."

"Of course we don't," said Lisa. "If Gregory and I learn something new together, I think it would work."

"Gregory," continued the counselor, "how would you feel about starting slowly to improve your relationship with Bernie? Perhaps you could ask if he would like to meet you at your club to shoot some baskets and work out? He might feel safer on neutral ground. Bernie's an athlete, and I bet you'd have a lot to show him. And Lisa, I think you need to let Gregory and Bernie know how painful this is for you. I bet you feel pulled in two different directions."

Lisa began to cry, and said, "These two guys are tearing me apart. I don't want to pick sides, but it feels like I'll lose my marriage if I allow Bernie to continue being so disrespectful to Gregory."

"Gregory and Lisa, if you would be willing to try my suggestions, I think we could include the children in our next session and learn how to hold family meetings. This is a time of adjustment for everyone. I realize you each did things differently before you got together, and that both of your methods worked. But now that you're all together, you'll need a plan you can agree on. If all of you would be willing to try some new things, the entire family would feel better." The Jordans agreed to try the counselor's suggestions before they did more damage to the relationships in the new family.

The Jordans aren't alone. Many families struggle with children who refuse to work or listen to a stepparent's requests simply because they don't want to be part of the new family. As the lack of cooperation increases, hurt feelings escalate. Instead of talking about their hurt feelings, stepparents often treat their stepchildren disrespectfully. And some children feel taken advantage of because they are expected to do chores in two different households. Trying to work out the problems without the involvement of the children is extremely difficult.

Working Out Step-Family Chore Problems at a Family Meeting

Whatever happens in a family affects everyone in different ways. When Ben Michaels and Sarah Robinson joined their families in a second marriage, they never dreamed that they or the children would encounter so many issues about family jobs. Ben's children lived full time with Ben and Sarah. They were independent and involved with family chores. Eight-year-old Adam was used to helping without complaining. Even two-year-old Francesca dressed herself and poured her own milk into her cereal from the miniature pitcher Ben provided for her.

Sarah's kids, fifteen-year-old Katie and ten-year-old Jonathan, lived with their father during the week and spent weekends with Ben and Sarah. When Sarah and her ex-husband Clint lived together, they had a maid and cleaning service. The children weren't expected to do any work at all. After the divorce, Clint quit his job to start a new business, which meant a big decrease in income. Clint expected his children to take care of the household chores while he developed his new business. After many difficulties during the five years following the divorce, the children took on more and more work around his house.

One weekend when Katie and Jonathan were at Ben and Sarah's place, Ben insisted they help with the yard work. He was tired of watching them relax while his children worked. Both Katie and Jonathan ignored Ben. Katie ran to her mother and said, "Ben just told us we have to help with the yard work. This isn't even our house. Just because you decided to marry Ben doesn't mean we're going to do what he says. He's not our father."

Sarah told her children, "I know Ben isn't your father, but he is a person who lives in this house and has rights just like the rest of us. I think of this house as belonging to everyone, even if you don't see it that way. I'm sorry you're so angry. I can't

make you help, but I'd feel a lot better if you could contribute when you're here." Katie stopped complaining, but she and Jonathan refused to help with the yard work and went inside to watch a video.

Ben continued to feel resentful. He didn't ask the children to help any more that day, but he complained vehemently to Sarah about how "spoiled" and "irresponsible" her children were. It hurt Sarah to hear Ben talk that way. She felt upset because she didn't think her children were spoiled or irresponsible, but she wanted Ben to be happy.

After Sarah's children returned to their father's, Adam asked his father, "How come Sarah's kids never have to do chores when they stay with us? It's not fair that we have to do all the work around here." Ben agreed it wasn't fair, but said that Sarah's kids refused to listen to him and Sarah wasn't going to do anything about it.

Sarah overheard the conversation. "Adam," she said, "you sound pretty angry about this."

"I sure am," he said. "Why don't you make your kids help out?"

Sarah thought for a moment and said, "I don't want to insist they work if they don't want to. I know they do a lot all week at their Dad's house, and I think they need a break on weekends."

"I think you're just afraid they'll stop coming over if you ask them to help," argued Ben. "Maybe I should go on strike and refuse to do anything for your kids until they pitch in around here."

Adam liked that idea, but Sarah said, "I know you're angry and I'm upset that my kids are being disrespectful, too, but that's too extreme! Ben, you may be right that I'm afraid the kids will stop coming over if I push more work on them. But you do have the right to expect cooperation. Instead of a strike, how about if we sit down as a family the next time they come and talk about what is happening?"

Family Meetings Provide a
Forum for Everyone

The next time Sarah's children were at the house, everyone sat down to discuss the chore problem. Sarah started the meeting by telling her children that Ben was so upset with their behavior that he was considering going on strike and refusing to help them until they decided to help the family. "I'm not in favor of a strike, but I also don't think it's right for us to do all the work. I would like to understand why you don't help when you're here. In fact, I think everyone in the family should have a chance to say what they think about this problem."

Adam spoke first. "I'm glad we're having a meeting. I'm really mad that I have to do so much work around here. Francesca is only two and can't do very many things yet, so I get stuck with everything. I don't think it's fair that you guys don't help when you're here. Sometimes when you leave, Sarah expects me to clean up your messes and that's not right. And I don't like sharing my bedroom with you, Jonathan, because you leave your stuff everywhere when you go back to your Dad's."

Katie said, "I don't think it's fair that you have to clean up after us, Adam. I'll make sure I pick up my things before I leave. But Ben, we have to work all week at Dad's house. We never get a break. Then when we come here and it's our weekend, you have a million things for us to do. We don't want to work all the time just because you do!"

"Yeah," said Jonathan, "but Adam, I'm sorry about leaving your room all messy. I wouldn't like someone doing that to my room."

Ben spoke up, "I have an idea. Are we ready for a solution?" Everyone nodded in agreement. "I do like to get a lot done on weekends, but I don't expect you to work the whole time you're here. How about each of you giving me an hour a day? I promise not to bug you the rest of the weekend." Sarah let out a sigh of relief. This was the first time she heard Ben sound reasonable. She was so worried that her children wouldn't want to come for weekends if they couldn't resolve this issue. She wanted to support Ben, but she thought he was expecting too much of the children.

Katie said an hour a day would be fine as long as she and Ben planned the time together so it didn't interfere with her part-time job, her boyfriend, or her homework. Jonathan thought an hour a day would be fun if he and Adam could work together. Ben assured the children he could schedule the work to meet their needs.

Two-year-old Francesca, who had been sitting quietly during the discussion, asked, "More ice cream?" Sarah and Ben exchanged smiles of relief, knowing their combined family had taken a first step toward more harmonious living.

Coordinating Schedules: A Challenge for Blended Families

Sometimes the problem isn't whether family members are willing to help, but rather whether they are available to help. In some families, members are rarely in the same place at the same time because of varying visitation schedules and active lifestyles. Sometimes finding ways to share the workload and create times everyone can work together just isn't possible.

If you are having a problem with schedules, try these tips:

1. Use signs, notes, and other nonverbal ways to make requests. A creative mother made a special envelope for each child with his or her name and photo on it. When the child was at the house, he or she found chore assignments inside the envelope. A family that used a large eraseable board to notify family members of work assignments told the following story:

"When we painted the inside of the house, all our routines fell apart for days. We thought it was because of the painting until our eight-year-old stepdaughter arrived for the weekend. She asked, 'Where's our erase board? I can't remember if I'm supposed to cook tonight or tomorrow.' We hadn't realized how much we depended on looking at the board to remind us of chores and routines. We put everything on that board— doctor's appointments, shopping lists, menu choices, car pool days, music lessons, sports events, the works. We put the board back up before we hung our pictures so we could get back to normal."

2. Create family work days once a month. You can usually find one day a month when everyone can get together. Make sure you have fun, too. Play lively music and plan a pizza party or ice cream sundae treat at the end of the day.

3. Agree on the amount of time each family member will work during the week and let each person work at his or her convenience.

4. Assign work by the percentage of time spent in the family. For example, if a stepchild stays at the house 10 percent of the time, he or she would be expected to contribute 10 percent of a full-time share.

5. Consider whether or not the job can wait until the person returns. If the job can't wait, the person whose job it is can arrange in advance to have another family member fill in. Someone can offer to do the job for the absent family member if that person is willing to make a trade or do something extra when he or she returns to the house. Sometimes family members are willing to do extra jobs for pay when negotiated in advance.

6. Consider including the position of "alternate" in job planning. The alternate fills in and does the jobs for absent family members for an agreed period of time. Set this up during the regular job planning process.

7. Try a check system. One family decided together that if a person forgot a chore before leaving for the other parent's home, he or she would get a check. After accumulating three checks, the person would do extra dishes for everyone the next time he or she was at the house.

As long as everyone agrees in advance, a system will usually work. If there are problems, put them on the agenda for the next family meeting.

Three other reasons often make inviting cooperation difficult. Perhaps one family member (or more) refuses to help at all because work isn't expected at their other home. Still others simply don't know how to do a job and are embarrassed to admit it. In other cases, children may feel competitive and refuse to do anything another family member can do better.

Motivating a Child Who Is Not Used to Helping Out

Making work a game can motivate an untrained, unskilled worker to get involved and make a contribution. John Becker's thirteen-year-old stepson Keith was a frequent dinner guest at the house. Keith was a bright, capable person. However, when it came time to clean up, John noticed that his stepson consistently disappeared.

The next time Keith came for dinner and pulled his disappearing act, John asked his wife Felice, "Where's Keith?"

"I don't know. Every time we have to clean up, he disappears. He doesn't have to help out at his father's house, so maybe he thinks it's all right to do the same here."

John went to find Keith to ask for his help. After he found him in his room playing a video game, John asked Keith why he didn't stay to help the family. Keith gave every excuse he could think of. After some prodding, John discovered the real problem: his stepson had never done a dish in his life and didn't know how. Too embarrassed to admit this at his age, he avoided helping instead.

John told his wife what he thought the problem was and asked if she'd mind his helping Keith get more involved.

"Are you kidding," she exclaimed, "if you can motivate him to do anything, it will be a miracle. He doesn't do a thing I ask."

John called Keith into the kitchen and said, "Did your mother ever tell you I was in the Revolutionary War?"

"Wasn't that a long time ago?" Keith asked.

"That's true, I was very young at the time, and all they would let me do were dishes. Let me show you a few tricks I learned as I washed dishes for thousands of soldiers day after day." Keith looked on with interest, even though he was pretty sure his stepfather wasn't really that old.

By making a game out of teaching Keith how to do dishes, John was able to help him save face and learn at the same time. John showed Keith how to use cleanser and a brillo pad to clean the broiler pan. "We used to use sand and rawhide, but these work almost as well," he teased.

A half hour later, after intense scrubbing, Keith produced the shiniest broiler pan in the family's history. Everyone raved about the great job. The next time he stayed for dinner, he jumped in to help, saying to his startled mother, "Let me show you some tricks John taught me that he learned doing dishes for the soldiers during the Revolutionary War."

Next, John asked Keith if he would like to learn some tricks from the Spanish-American War.

"You were in that one, too," Keith exclaimed. "I didn't even know you were a soldier."

"Well Keith, I have to admit I didn't do any fighting because they kept me so busy in the kitchen. It was in that war that I really learned how to cook. Want me to teach you?"

"Sure," said Keith enthusiastically.

"Let's start by making your lunch for school. Now you could do a simple peanut butter sandwich, but the troops used to like something with a little more pizzaz. My specialty was called 'The Dagwood of all Dagwoods Sandwich.' First you shave some lettuce real thin. Then you cut green peppers into perfect rounds. The troops always liked hot peppers and onions, but they might give you indigestion. What do you think?"

"I want to make my sandwich just like you do, John."

"Okay. Then pay close attention," John continued. "I learned to spread the mustard and mayo with a spatula because it went faster. Then I heap the lettuce, onions, green peppers, and hot peppers on like so. Next, I throw on some slices of your favorite lunch meat. The troops used to love buffalo, but they don't carry it at the grocery store so we'll have to settle for turkey. Now comes my secret ingredient. I sprinkle just a little vinegar on. You've got to be careful not to use too much, or the bread gets soggy and the troops complain. Hey, these look good enough to eat. What do you say, shall we have a snack and make some new ones for your lunch?"

Keith knew that John hadn't been in any of the wars he talked about. In fact, he suspected John learned how to make his sandwich by watching the kid who worked at the deli down the street. But he liked learning from John because he made everything fun. Soon Keith was cooking dinners for the family regularly, as well as helping John do the grocery shopping.

In another situation, a young girl named Louise refused to cook when at her father's house because her stepsister made fun of her and criticized her efforts. Her stepsister was an excellent cook who got compliments on everything she made, but felt threatened by competition. Louise, figuring she couldn't compete, said she hated cooking and refused to help with that chore. At her mother's house, however, Louise cooked almost every day to avoid her mother's specialties: fried foods, gravies, grade "D" meats—anything high in fat. Louise was taking a nutrition class at her high school and didn't want to eat foods her teacher said were unhealthy.

Parents blending families aren't the only ones with problems to solve. Single parents tell us they are overwhelmed and exhausted trying to juggle everything. Even if it was only an illusion, they thought they had someone to turn to for help before their divorce or death of a spouse. Now they find living alone with the children isolating and difficult.

Other Issues Single Parents Struggle With

If you are a single parent, do you worry that your children have to grow up too fast because of the extra responsibilities you give them to help make the family work? Do you sometimes find it easier to do everything yourself because teaching the children a new routine takes too long? Do you feel overwhelmed because there's just too much for one person to do? Do you occasionally take this out on your children?

Jim, a single father of two, sixteen-year-old Sammy and fourteen-year-old Jane, struggled with these issues. Jim's two teens lived with him except for occasional visits with their mother, who took them on trips to fabulous resorts or on special fun outings such as sporting events and concerts. In an effort to make sure his children learned to be responsible, Jim created a routine that worked smoothly, except for minor irritations when one child felt the work was divided unevenly. Usually problems were discussed at family meetings, and everyone helped solve them. Jim's routine changed when his company sent him back to school to retrain for a new program. After working all day, attending classes evenings, and trying to keep up with his homework, he had no patience for problem solving or family meetings. He snapped at his children and insisted they take on extra work because he was too busy. He resented the time his children spent with their mother, because they were off having fun while he was home slaving away.

Jane and Sammy were responsible and did their best to help out, but Jim's expectations were impossible. The teens, tired of trying to pick up the slack, decided to write a letter to their dad, when they couldn't pin him down for family meeting.

After debating what to write, Jane and Sammy composed the following letter and gave it to their father.

Dear Dad,

We want to help you out, but you are taking advantage of us. We wish you had a wife to help you with the extra work. We think you are dumping everything on us because we are the only ones here. You are putting too much on us. When you ask us to do your jobs, we get frustrated because we can't say no and argue with you. Then we all get in some kind of fight about something little or just don't talk for about two or three hours. It happens practically every day, and although we try to be nice, we can't be because you treat us like slaves.

We could work this problem out together if we had a family meeting, but since you are too busy to meet with us, we have three ideas. They are better than nothing at all or us being mad at each other all the time.

Our first suggestion is that when you come in the house, you should say "hi" before you start giving us a list of things to do. Our second suggestion is that we could have a counseling session to figure out a way for us to stop getting on each other's nerves. Our third suggestion is that maybe we could set a work time on the weekend when we could help each other with the extra jobs.

All of these solutions can work very well, but we all need to agree on what we will do, because your tone of voice and timing just isn't going to work. We definitely can't keep going on like we are now, always coming home annoying each other all the time. It just doesn't work. We hope you can agree with one of these choices. Maybe we can talk about this soon.

Love always,

Jane and Sammy

When Jim read the letter, he realized he had lost sight of what a parent's role is and what a child's is. He knew he had been ordering his teens around because he was so stressed. He didn't think what he was doing was fair, but he was desperate because he couldn't think of anyone else to ask for help. Jim realized that he had been thinking only of himself. He decided to take a break from his homework and talk with his children.

After apologizing for his behavior, Jim asked if he could add some suggestions to the list the children had started.

"Great, Dad. All we want to do is solve the problem. What are your ideas?"

Jim said, "We could agree on an amount of time each person would work during the week, do what we can, and let the rest go. Or maybe we could hire someone to do my chores."

"Dad, you know you can't afford to hire someone. How about we each put in an hour a week whenever we have time, and then we could work together for an hour on the weekend to finish what is left," suggested Sammy.

"Great idea. Let's do it. And thanks for writing me such a great letter. Your old dad seems to have gone temporarily insane, but I'll get better with your help." Everyone laughed.

Then Sammy said, "Dad, we know how busy you are, but we miss having fun with you like we used to. Remember when we played 'Make-Me-Laugh' at the dinner table? That didn't take much time, but it was fun trying to get everybody to laugh. Remember the time Jane and I wouldn't laugh until you poured syrup over your head? We didn't stop laughing for a week. Could we play that again soon?"

"How about right now?" Jim started making faces.

"Come on, Dad," said Jane, "you can do better than that!"

It's easy to take advantage of capable children when you are a single parent. Even if you don't want your children to assume all the work, it's tempting to allow it when you are at work or involved in activities away from home. Your children may even be more skilled at doing housework than you are, because they were more involved before the divorce or death. Remember that they are just kids and it's not their job to pick up your slack.

Another difficulty for single parents is working things out with their ex-partner. Sometimes two people who were married can be friends who cooperate in the interest of the children. Other times there is no communication at all. And in most cases, there are difficulties and disagreements to work out.

Working Out Issues with Ex-Partners

Brad's ex-wife Wendy ran her home like an army barrack. When the children stayed with their father, Wendy called regularly to insist that Brad follow the routines she did. She pushed all his guilt buttons when she said the children were confused by the inconsistencies.

Brad didn't want to make it hard for his children, so he tried to do things the way Wendy did. Wendy wanted Brad to give the children allowance only if they did all their work. Brad didn't think it was a good idea to connect chores with money. He thought it was a better idea to pay the children for extra jobs he would hire someone to do and give them their allowance so they could learn to deal with money. But Wendy insisted that, even though they were divorced, his job as a father was to help her parent the children consistently so they didn't get confused.

One morning Brad's daughter refused to clear the table. Although she was running late, she didn't like the outfit she picked and wanted to change before the school bus came. "You look just fine the way you are," said Brad. "If you don't clear the table, I'm deducting money from your allowance."

"That's not fair. You said we could have an allowance to buy things we need. Besides, taking it away is punishment, and you said you don't believe in punishment."

"I don't care what I said, just clear that table and stop arguing."

"No I won't. I don't care if you give me an allowance or not. I'm going to change my clothes and catch the bus."

Brad felt miserable all day because of the fight with his daughter. He couldn't concentrate on a thing at work. During a coffee break, Brad told a coworker about Wendy's demands and their fight.

"Brad," she asked, "do you think our competitors do everything exactly the way we do in our company?"

"Of course not. We all have different ways of operating." Brad paused then added, "Oh, I get it. Are you saying it's okay if Wendy does things her way and I do things my way?"

"Of course it is," said his friend. "Your differences were probably one of the reasons you and Wendy didn't stay together. Now you have your own place and you need to find out what works for you."

Brad heaved a sigh of relief. He couldn't believe he had lost sight of such a simple truth. He called his ex-wife. "Wendy, I've been thinking about something. Every family has different rules and different ways of doing things. At your house you do things your way, and that's your business. But at my house, I've been trying to do things your way, too, and it isn't working for me. From now on, I'm going to do things my way at my house. The kids will figure out that there are different ways to do things and won't be confused if you and I don't criticize each other."

"Brad, parents must present a united front or their children will be permanently damaged," argued Wendy.

"I know you have the best interests of the children in mind, but I don't agree with what you are saying. It would be better for all of us if you would stop pressuring me to do things your way. That's not a good message for the children. We have two different houses now and two different families and two different ways of doing things. I know it may take a little time to make the transition, but our children are very capable, and they'll work it out."

Brad wasn't sure if Wendy liked his suggestion, but he was certain that it was all right to be himself with his children.

When his daughter came home later that day, he asked, "When did you start feeling better after our fight this morning? I've been miserable all day."

She smiled and said, "I stopped being mad as soon as I got on the bus with my friends, but I still don't think it's right for you to punish me by taking away my allowance."

"I agree with you. I was under a lot of pressure this morning, and I made a mistake threatening you like that. I'm not going to take away your allowance."

Brad's daughter gave him a big hug and said, "Did you clear the table for me this morning? Maybe I could do your job tonight."

"That would be really nice," said Brad.

Even with pressure from Wendy, Brad decided to focus on what worked for him. Change is a slow process, and Brad made mistakes along the way, but he was capable of learning from his errors when no one was standing on the sidelines judging him.

Mistakes: Wonderful Opportunities To Learn and Grow

Your children can learn from mistakes, too. When you meet the challenges of divorce or death, your "children can learn that they can handle whatever life presents with courage and optimism. They can see the opportunity to learn and grow from experiences instead of seeing problems as failures."[1] If you remember to focus on progress instead of perfection, you will be amazed at how well your family can handle the after-effects of divorce or death. You don't need to rush; just let the process unfold and use the suggestions in this chapter to help you through the rough spots.

---

1. *Positive Discipline A–Z* by Jane Nelsen, Lynn Lott, and H. Stephen Glen. (Rocklin, CA: Prima Publishing, 1993), p. 128.

CHAPTER 10

Meeting the Challenges of Adults Living Together

In the beginning of this book we described a family as a group of people living together in a household. Until now, our focus has been on families with children. This chapter offers help to those of you who live in or wish to create an all-adult household, including roommate situations and couples adjusting to the empty nest. We'll also explore helpful suggestions for families taking on the responsibility of caring for an elderly parent.

We suggest you start by reading the entire book, as the suggestions throughout *Chores Without Wars* can be modified to work in all-adult households. Solving problems will be easy if you are fortunate enough to live with people who are motivated to cooperate. If you are the only person who wants improvement, your work will be more difficult, but you can still use the ideas in this book to invite others to join you. Because we believe that a home should be safe and comfortable for all family members, we offer alternatives to putting up with uncomfortable or disrespectful situations.

Dealing with Adult Roommate Situations

We found that households that were "stuck together" instead of formed with intention had the most difficulty with cooperation. Young college people who moved away from home and formed households for the first time resisted structure and advice to formulate an organized plan. The housemates didn't want to be "bossed" now that they no longer lived at home.

Cooperation was impossible when roommates handled conflict by staying with a friend or avoiding contact completely. If the living arrangement was for a short time, housemates were less motivated to work things out, saying they could put up with the problems for the time involved.

The households that met with the most success were those in which people looked for a living situation that met their needs or formed a household with like-minded people. Whatever the motivation for sharing a household, it was extremely important to have a way of resolving the inevitable conflicts. Without that, house members were stuck grinning and bearing a bad situation or doing everything alone.

You can do little to improve a situation if the others involved don't want to change. For that reason we recommend you carefully check out the situation first to make sure it will be compatible with your needs. Look for household members who are willing to talk about issues and feelings and have a sincere desire to work things out. Since avoiding problems completely is impossible, it is important that potential housemates have both the desire and the tools to work out difficulties. Use the pointers below to select a situation that will work for you.

Pointers for Finding Compatible Roommate Situations

1. Look for ads posted where people with interests similar to yours gather.

2. Meet and talk with potential roommates to find out more about them. Ask about their interests and daily living habits (especially concerning noise, messiness, pets, and TV), the actual cost of living in the household, and ideas about sharing those costs.

3. Find out whose name is on the lease and how people can leave if they aren't satisfied. If your name is on the lease and others leave, you are obligated to find new roommates or cover the costs yourself. Make sure you have a say in accepting or rejecting new roommates.

4. Make sure you are starting with people who want to cooperate and work toward win/win solutions when you check out the new household. Find out if current household members have an established structure for resolving conflicts or would be willing to create one.

In the stories below, roommates demonstrated the importance of having both skills and goodwill to help each other deal with issues as they came up. It wasn't always easy to be open and honest, but they found that the more they talked about issues, the easier it was to work out difficulties.

Sharing Gripes Respectfully Improves Roommate Situations

Valerie thought it was a great idea when Gwen and Seth asked her to share an off-campus apartment with them. She looked forward to being out of the dorm and living on her own. Because she liked Gwen and Seth and was able to talk easily with them, she thought they'd all get along well.

They moved in together and began setting up a household. Their first joint decision was to share food. They planned to shop together and split the bill. The next week at the scheduled time, Gwen said, "Oh, I forgot, I can't go today. They gave me an extra shift at work and I have to get ready. You don't mind if I don't go with you, do you?"

Valerie and Seth both said, "I guess not," and left to do the shopping. At the store they realized they would have to advance Gwen's share of the money for groceries. Even though Gwen paid them back later, it was inconvenient because they didn't have enough money in their accounts and had to make an extra trip to the bank to deposit Gwen's money. When this happened three weeks in a row, Valerie and Seth began to resent it.

Gwen had resentments, too. She approached Valerie a few days after the shopping was done and said, "I was going to make a sandwich, but all the cheese is gone! What happened to it?"

Valerie replied, "I didn't have any. I think Seth had friends over and made grilled cheese sandwiches. They must have finished it."

Gwen made a face and said, "That's not fair. Seth and his friends eat half the food in the house!"

Valerie replied, "It's true he eats way more than we do. I don't think our food arrangement is working. Seth and I also have some issues about the grocery shopping we haven't shared with you. We need to talk about what's going on."

The three housemates sat down to talk that evening. They all agreed things weren't working as planned and they needed to make some changes. Seth suggested that they share foods like milk, eggs, bread, jam, and condiments, but keep the rest of the food separate.

They tried Seth's idea for a few weeks, but problems continued to arise. They realized this system wasn't working either, so they agreed it would be best for each of them to do their shopping and keep their food separate. They divided the refrigerator and cabinet space. Each person bought his or her own groceries and put them in a designated place. If one cooked and wanted to share, he or she could, but there were no expectations. Except for occasional emergency pilfering that no one seemed to mind, this plan worked best.

Once the food problem was resolved, the three roommates focused on the problems related to cleaning. Originally, everyone agreed to clean together every two weeks. They made a sign-up sheet where each could initial the job selected, then add the date after it was completed. The women noticed they were doing most of the cleaning and decided to talk to Seth.

Valerie began, "Seth you're never around at cleaning time."

Gwen added, "Yeah, and if you are here, you're being a couch potato. We're doing all the cleaning."

Seth agreed with them and said, "Between work and school, I hardly have any time for myself. I hate to spend it cleaning. I know it has to be done, and I appreciate that you've both been picking up the slack. What I'd like to do is take on the major cleaning at the end of the quarter. I'll scrub the floors, do the windows, move the furniture, vacuum, and stuff like that to make up for my part."

The women agreed, and at the end of the quarter, Seth followed through and did a thorough cleaning. He scrubbed the floors and the bathroom tub and toilet, moved the furniture and vacuumed, washed the windows, and cleaned the oven. It took him an entire weekend, but when he was finished, the apartment sparkled. Everyone was happy with the way they solved the problem.

Sometimes it takes experimenting with different strategies to come up with one that works for everybody. It's important to focus on solutions instead of looking for who to blame for the problem. Here's another creative solution to a problem a family of roommates struggled with.

A group of college grads decided to share a household to cut down on expenses and enjoy each others' company. They spent hours working out issues of communal living and tried to reach consensus on every topic. They had a job wheel for daily chores, a home improvement day once every three months for bigger projects, and a weekly potluck so everyone could get together for fun. For the most part, the household ran smoothly, but one problem they couldn't seem to resolve was the recurring toilet paper shortage.

First, everyone figured the "tissue issue" would take care of itself; then they argued over who bought it last; next they tried taking turns buying; then they tried a chart. Nothing worked. The inability to solve this simple problem was breaking down family unity. Arguments erupted that started with "I always . . . ," "You never . . . ," "How come so and so doesn't . . . ," and on and on. After several meetings with no progress, one household member got tired of the debate and said, "Look, everyone give me $5. I'll find out where I can buy a case of toilet paper so we don't have to discuss this again. Our friendships are too important for all this petty bickering." He came home with a case of ninety-six rolls of toilet paper, and that solved the problem for months. His housemates were relieved to find a solution that ended their bickering about what was fair or who was to blame.

In the previous situations people were able to talk and work out their problems. At times talking doesn't help. Someone may be giving a double message, saying one thing and doing something else. When a situation arises where someone continually promises to do a job and doesn't follow through, it's important to "listen" to their actions instead of to their words.

Tolerating Double Messages Impedes Cooperation

Andy was a freshman living in a college dorm. He and his roommate Brad shared a room. It didn't take long for Andy to realize that he and Brad had different standards of cleanliness. Andy came from a family where everyone pitched in weekly to keep the house clean and orderly. If there was a problem, the family discussed it and worked out a solution. Brad was used to having things done for him and wasn't interested in picking up after himself.

One day, when the room was almost impassable, Andy suggested Brad pick up his stuff from the floor so that he could vacuum.

Brad responded, "Hey, I'll get to it later. Just vacuum around my stuff." Brad never got to it. Andy found that if he pushed Brad's stuff under his bed, he could vacuum the floor once a week. This way he could take care of himself, not build resentment, and not expect that Brad would change.

It is easy to believe what people say, like Andy did, but the real test is to pay attention to what people do. People may convey good intentions with their words, but their actions tell the truth about what they are willing to do. If you want to truly understand people, pay more attention to what they do than to what they say.[1] Dan James learned this the hard way in our next story.

Dan and Gary were friends in school. They found jobs in the same town and decided to share an apartment. Shortly after they were settled, Dan started to notice he had an uneasy feeling about going home each night. The house was getting messier and messier, and he almost hated to walk in the door. One evening when he went into the kitchen and saw the pile of dishes and pots Gary left, he felt his stomach tighten.

He walked into the living room where Gary was watching TV and asked, "Gary, when are you going to get the dishes done? I'd like to make my dinner but there's a pile of dirty dishes in the sink."

Gary responded, "Oh, I forgot. I'll get them done in a little while, after this show is over."

Dan remembered saying things like that to his mother when he was a teenager. He didn't think he was being too demanding, but he felt uneasy just the same. Instead of making an issue out of Gary's procrastination, Dan went back into the kitchen, made his dinner, and cleaned up around the piles of

---

1. For more information on the difference between actions and words and how to effectively deal with double messages, read *Positive Discipline for Parenting in Recovery* by Jane Nelsen, Riki Intner, and Lynn Lott (Rocklin, CA: Prima Publishing, 1992).

dishes. He was thinking about all the other times he had washed all the dishes for Gary, and he felt his anger rise. The next morning before he left for work, Dan noticed the same piles of dishes in the sink.

A few days later Dan was getting his clothes ready to take to the cleaners. Gary walked in and said, "I'm going to the cleaners before work. Just leave your clothes and I'll take them in with mine."

Dan thought, "Maybe I've been unfair and too hard on Gary. He's really a nice guy."

That night when Dan came home, his clothes were where he'd left them. He was angry and asked, "What happened? I thought you were going to the cleaners."

"I ran short of time. I was late for work and decided to do it tomorrow. Don't worry, I'll get it done then."

The next evening Dan again found his clothes where he had left them. Dan promised himself he would never believe

what Gary said again. Later that day, Dan discussed the situation with a friend at work who said, "Dan, it looks as if Gary's words don't match his actions. His behavior is the reality, not his promises. You trust his words and end up disappointed. You need to tell him you aren't going to take promises anymore."

That evening the sink was filled with dirty dishes again. Dan asked Gary to turn off the TV because he had something important to say. When he told Gary about the dishes, he heard, "I'm going to do them before I go to bed."

"Gary," Dan said, "I don't take promises any more. Don't tell me, show me."

Gary looked surprised, "What do you mean?"

"I'm more interested in good actions than good intentions. From now on, don't say it. Just do it!" Then Dan walked out of the room without further comment.

Every time Gary started to make a promise about doing something, Dan told him that wasn't acceptable because he wanted action, not words

One evening Dan came home and found the storage locker had been left open. Gary was eating dinner when Dan came in and said, "The storage locker was left open. I'm concerned our stuff may be taken."

Gary started, "Oh, I . . . ," then paused before he said, "I know. You want action." He got up and locked the cabinet. He'd finally gotten the message.

Dan and Gary demonstrated their intention to work things out. Without the desire to change, nothing would have improved. Had Dan not found a solution, this problem could have escalated into a hostile confrontation or a scene where one roommate would be forced to leave.

In some families people don't communicate at all, so it is difficult to work anything out. A young woman moved into a large house with fifteen other people to be closer to her boyfriend. For weeks, none of the others realized she was living there, because so many people came and went on different schedules. People pilfered food from each other, slept in a bed if the owner wasn't home without asking permission, and resisted all efforts to plan formal meetings. There were a lot of resentments but no formal process for resolving them. If someone had a complaint, he or she put a hostile or sarcastic note on the refrigerator. People reading the note felt criticized, attacked, and defensive.

If you are living with others who refuse to talk, we suggest you look for another place where people are willing to treat each other with respect and talk over differences. You may need to ask an uncooperative or difficult roommate to leave for the same reasons. We emphasize the principles of mutual respect, open communication, and shared decision making, which apply whether you live with a group of people you have just met or with family members.

Creating New Patterns When Children Leave Home

Trudy started attending parenting classes when Ali was three and Mary was five. She and her husband Chuck attended classes together and worked hard to teach the girls new skills. Over the years the family established a cooperative way of handling the household work. Things went smoothly, even through adolescence.

When Mary left for college, the family was faced with having to reevaluate their situation and make adjustments. The household tasks that Mary handled had to be reassigned. Chuck, Trudy, and Ali realized that with the "work force" shrinking, they would each have to take on more. Chuck volunteered to get take-out food on Tuesdays, the night Mary made dinner. Ali said she'd be willing to clean the upstairs bathroom on cleaning day and set the table on the nights she was home.

Trudy told them she appreciated their willingness to pitch in. She offered to feed their dog Squirt and handle the trips to the vet. They all realized how much each family member was contributing to make their household run smoothly.

When Ali moved into an apartment two years later, Trudy and Chuck found themselves having to adjust once again. They decided how they could divide things up so neither was overburdened. Chuck picked another night to cook dinner and they decided to go out once a week. Trudy said she'd set the table. Since both Trudy and Chuck worked full time, they decided to hire someone to clean house. Trudy jokingly remarked that having the girls leave was hard since she and Chuck had come to rely on their help to keep the family running. With experienced workers like their daughters, things seemed to happen automatically.

When Mary and Ali came home for visits, Trudy and Chuck noticed that everyone naturally fell into the family routines set up a long time before. Mary set the table before dinner; after the meal, Ali cleared the table just like when she had lived at home. Trudy beamed, realizing that the years of training and working together really did pay off.

One night Trudy and Chuck rushed out to an early movie, leaving the kitchen a mess. They returned to find their daughters chattering away about their work and friends as they stood at the kitchen sink washing their parents' dinner dishes. When Chuck asked, "What's going on?" Ali replied, "The dishes were piled up and I knew you'd be back late, so Mary and I thought we'd do them for you." Chuck gave his girls a big hug and thanked them profusely.

Mary and Ali moved into their own places after leaving home and didn't come back to live in the household. Some children who leave home return after a while. In fact, one family had grown children coming and going so often that they joked about installing a revolving door. Many children spend summers or vacations between college semesters or seasonal jobs with the family. Some children return home to save money for an adventure or a place of their own.

Sometimes a divorce initiates a return home, perhaps even with young children in tow. If you don't set boundaries or practice mutual respect by thinking about your needs as well as your children's, you could end up in the awkward situation of having to ask your children to leave.

Monitoring the Revolving Door
When Children Come and Go

After a year of sharing an apartment with his friend, Rob Parker decided to move back home with his parents for a few months to catch up on his bills. Rob moved back into his old room and into some old habits. He "borrowed" things from his Dad, like clothes or tools, and didn't return them promptly. He made a lot of promises to pitch in and help, but he didn't follow through on what he said he'd do.

Rob asked to borrow his Dad's car one Friday night. As Mr. Parker debated whether to let Rob use his car, Rob said, "I'll wash it this weekend. Looks like it could use it." Mr. Parker decided to let him use the car. Monday morning when he left for work, he noticed it was still dirty.

The next morning as Mr. Parker was getting ready for work, he said to his wife, "I can't find my blue tie. Did you take it to the cleaners?"

"No, I saw Rob wearing it yesterday."

Mr. Parker exclaimed, "I can't believe he still has my tie. He told me he'd return it after he wore it last week. Why do I let him borrow my things? He never washed the car like he said he would either. I can't trust him, and I'm sick of this. I'm going to have to talk to that boy."

Trusting People to Be Who They Are

"I trusted you!" is what people say who feel their trust has been betrayed. We suggest you trust people to be who they are instead of living in hope that the person will be someone else. Mr. Parker was disappointed and hoped his son would behave differently. His wife offered to call cousin Bernice to see how she handled a similar problem with her son a few years back.

Mr. Parker's cousin Bernice was glad to share her solution. Whenever her son borrowed something, she asked for collateral, that is, something he needed or something that was important to him. She kept it until the borrowed item was returned, which she said was usually when promised. Mr. Parker decided to try her idea out with Rob.

The following day Rob asked to borrow his Dad's brown sweater, promising to return it the next morning.

Mr. Parker said, "I want some collateral first."

Rob asked, "What do you mean?"

"Give me your favorite CD. I'll keep it until I get my sweater back."

The next day Rob asked his Dad for his CD and handed him his brown sweater, along with a belt he had borrowed earlier that week.

By asking for collateral, Mr. Parker trusted Rob to be who he was and developed a plan to take care of himself. He continued to use collateral whenever Rob borrowed something from him. On one occasion he had collected his son's left dress shoe, car keys, and address book.

Even though Mr. Parker was working out some improvements with Rob, he was not happy with how comfortable Rob had become living back at home. He noticed that Rob wasn't paying his bills or saving money. One night he called a meeting for the family and expressed his concern.

Setting Time Limits on How Long
Family Members Stay

"Rob," Mr. Parker began, "your mother and I love you enough to set a limit on how long you can stay here. We don't think we're helping you be responsible by providing free room and board so we'd like you to find another place by the end of the month. If you need our help, we'll be glad to go looking for places with you." Rob responded by saying he was planning a move soon anyway, and it was okay.

It was difficult for the Parkers to ask Rob to leave. Once he was settled in his new place, they redecorated his old room as a combination guest room and study. Mrs. Parker moved her computer in and Mr. Parker set up his aquarium. They had asked Rob if he would like his old furniture, either to use or to sell so he could buy something for his new place. Rob was shocked to see his room dismantled, but he knew his parents were right to do it.

You have a right to a life without children and should not feel obligated to continue providing for them when they become adults. If you want to help your adult children for a short time but do not want them to become permanent household residents and dependent on you, let them know your limitations before they move in. If you enjoy having your adult children live with you, make sure you establish a way to work out difficulties together and to clarify agreements instead of operating by assumptions and innuendos.

Adult children aren't the only ones who are moving back home these days. People live longer today than ever before, and the average life expectancy continues to increase. That leaves many middle-aged children asking the question: "What will happen to my parents? Will I ever have one or both of them living with me?" In the coming years, many of you will answer yes. This chapter can help you with that experience.

The Challenge of Adding Elderly Parents to the Family

Whether you find yourself living under the same roof with an elderly parent because of financial circumstances, health reasons, or because you want to, many issues are involved. How you handle these issues is critical to the relationship you'll have with your parent. Living with an aging parent can be either a difficult and frustrating experience or a rich and rewarding one.

Carl Kassel had three sons and one daughter, Ethel Hopkins. Carl and his sons lived in Wisconsin, and Ethel lived in California. Ethel got calls from her brothers periodically saying their Dad was having increasing difficulty living alone. Finally her oldest brother called to say he and the other brothers had decided it would be best for Carl to move to California and live with Ethel. "After all," he said, "you are his daughter and we've looked after him all these years."

Ethel told her husband Harry what her brother had said. She was feeling guilty about being so far away from her father all these years and wanted him to come to live with them. Although he had his reservations, because Carl was not an easy man, Harry agreed.

Carl and his black lab, Bounder, moved in with Ethel and Harry and proceeded to make themselves at home. Carl sat in front of the TV most of the time and expected Ethel to wait on him. Bounder whined at the door for hours, but Carl just yelled at him to shut up instead of walking him. Since the Hopkins' yard wasn't fenced in, Bounder had nowhere to run without supervision. Harry felt so sorry for the dog that he started taking him on daily walks. Ethel worked full time and did most of the cooking, cleaning, and shopping. Harry would help out when asked. Carl expressed no interest in helping around the house and treated Ethel like she was the maid. He was extremely critical to boot.

A few months after he arrived, Carl was exceptionally vocal at dinner one night. "Ethel what did you do to this meat? I can't chew it. You know I hate broccoli, and these potatoes are runny. I can't eat this stuff." Ethel burst into tears.

"Now what are you crying about?" Carl continued, "You're just like your mother. You cry at the drop of a hat." He got up and left the table.

Harry tried to comfort his wife and said, "You don't deserve to be treated this way."

Ethel said, "I can't take this any more. I do his laundry, cook, and clean. All he does is complain and criticize. Yesterday I asked if he could wash his coffee cup out, and by the look he gave me, you'd think I committed a crime. He doesn't do anything to help out, even when I ask him to."

Ethel called her older brother and told him things weren't working out.

"I was afraid this might happen. I'll call the other brothers and get back to you," he said. They all agreed to chip in to cover the cost of an apartment in a retirement community where Carl could be provided with the services he required.

Perhaps even under the best of circumstances, Ethel and Harry would have been unable or unwilling to deal with Carl. Had they considered the points on the following list, though, they may have created a more workable situation for the elderly parent. Examine these suggestions before adding an elderly parent to your home.

Five Tips to Consider When Adding Elderly Parents to Your Home

1. **Be clear about your boundaries.** What jobs are you willing and able to do, what jobs need to be hired out (including nursing care), and what do you expect your parent to do? What are your guidelines for pets, smoking, drinking, and visi-

tors? How much room is there for negotiation about these requirements?

2. **Be clear about defining space.** What rooms are available to your parent? Where and when will family members watch TV? What routines does the family have that won't be changing (such as overnights with friends, birthday parties, trips away from home)?

3. **Set up a forum, such as a weekly family meeting, for working out problems and handling complaints and criticism.** Make sure your parent knows he or she will be invited to be part of family decision making and that his or her input is crucial.

4. **Find out your parent's special skills and focus on positive ways to be involved and significant in the family.** Let your parent know where he or she can help pick up the slack or trade services. Be clear with your parent that he or she will be a family member, not a guest, in your household.

5. **Create activities the family can do together for fun and closeness.** Include new rituals and routines like a special dinner once a week or an outing on weekends or a day to look through picture albums together. Get input from your parent about activities he or she enjoys that the family could join.

The Harris family was able to use many of the pointers on the list, thus creating ways for Clare's mother to fit in without disrupting the entire family. Clare and Walter Harris had two children, Martin, nineteen, and Helen, seventeen. Martin was away at college and Helen was starting her senior year. Clare and Walter had talked about moving to a smaller house after Helen graduated from high school. They wondered why they should keep a large house just for two of them.

Irene, Walter's seventy-eight-year-old mother, had lived alone for the past seven years after her husband died. She kept herself busy with her different interests and activities. While visiting Irene, Clare noticed some alarming changes in her mother-in-law. Once an excellent housekeeper, Irene seemed to be slowing down. Clare noticed a grime buildup in the bathroom, the kitchen garbage filled to overflowing, and dirty dishes stacked at the sink. Some of the "clean" dishes in the cupboard looked as if they could use a going over. Clare washed the dishes and took the garbage to the dumpster on her way to the car. She decided to talk with her husband that evening and share her concerns.

"Honey," Clare began, "I'm very concerned about your mother."

"What do you mean?" Walter asked.

"I stopped by to see her and noticed her house isn't the way she used to keep it. The tub was grimy, the garbage was full, and the dishes were dirty. That's just not like her. I don't think she can really take care of herself."

Helen overheard their conversation and added, "I stopped by Gram's last week and she told me the same story three times. At first I thought she was fooling around, but she really didn't know she was repeating herself."

Walter thought for a little while then sighed, "So what are you saying?"

Clare said, "It's becoming harder for your mother to live alone. Let's be realistic and face facts, and think about what we can do."

"She'll never go into one of those homes for old people. She said she'd die first."

Clare responded, "I'm not talking about a nursing home, but we have to deal with this and consider our options."

A few weeks later when Irene was visiting with the Harrises she asked, "What are you going to do when Helen leaves for school? This is such a big house for just the two of you."

Clare replied, "Oh, I don't know. We were talking about moving into something smaller."

"Oh," Irene sighed then got quiet.

Later that night Walter remarked, "I wonder what my mother meant by that comment about our house."

"Do you think she was hinting that she'd like to live here? You know how hard it is for your mother to be direct."

"How do you feel about my mother moving in? Is it even a possibility?"

"I suppose so. The house is large and we could fix up the downstairs room for your mom." After more discussion they got input from the kids and were ready to talk to Irene.

Initially she was reluctant, but she decided to make the move after she found out her good friend was being placed in a nursing home. They talked together about what Irene should bring, where they could put her things, and what items could be sold at a garage sale. Irene moved into a comfortable room and had many familiar items around to help her feel more at home. The Harrises involved her in their regularly scheduled family meetings and encouraged her to put items on the agenda. They decided to have a cleaning day on Saturdays. Helen liked to sleep in, so they set the work time from 10:00 A.M. to 2:00 P M.

As the family was doing the Saturday cleaning, Clare noticed her mother-in-law was looking tired as she pushed the vacuum. "Mom, why don't you switch with me and sit and fold the towels. I could use a break." Irene sat down and folded for fifteen minutes, which allowed her to catch her breath. She got up and began dusting, swaying to the beat of Helen's new CD.

Walter did the family's grocery shopping on Mondays. He asked his mother to help him with it because she always picked out such wonderful produce. While they were out, he noticed Irene was looking tired. Walter suggested they take a break and get some frozen yogurt. After the break, Irene was able to continue shopping. Irene didn't have the stamina and energy she once did, but she wouldn't speak up for fear of inconveniencing her family. Walter and Clare were sensitive to this and planned accordingly.

Helen was scheduled to cook one evening when she noticed her grandmother sitting in her room. "Gram, would you tell me how to cook those wonderful mashed potatoes you used to make?"

Irene went into the kitchen with Helen and started rattling off the ingredients and explained how to prepare the potatoes.

Helen was excited. "Would you be willing to work with me on my night to cook and teach me how to make all the things I loved to eat at your house?"

Irene beamed and said, "Of course. I'll get the ingredients when I go shopping with your Dad."

"Great! Can we make those little cookies with the jelly in the middle? We could surprise Mom and Dad with them."

The Harrises found many opportunities to help Irene feel important, useful, and appreciated. They looked for ways to involve Irene in the household work so she could remain connected and make a contribution to the family.

Problems still came up from time to time. One day Irene complained to Clare about Helen's loud music. Clare suggested Irene put it on the agenda and bring it up at their weekly meeting. When she did, Helen complained that Irene had the TV on every afternoon when she came home from school. It was difficult to have friends over and have to listen to soap operas, so she played her music to drown out the TV.

After some lively discussion, Irene agreed to use the small TV in her room in the afternoons, and Helen agreed to keep the volume of her music lowered. Both were relieved to meet their needs without disturbing the other.

The family found that they could deal with the problems that came up and maintain respect for everyone. They were able to talk about their expectations and different styles and work on solutions to problems instead of blaming and arguing. They were fortunate that Irene was willing to talk at their meetings and share her feelings and ideas. They knew that some older people are unaccustomed and unwilling to address issues directly, making it difficult or impossible to resolve issues.

Whether you are or are thinking of living with roommates, adult children, or elderly parents, we hope the ideas in this chapter make your situation more positive for everyone. There is nothing more satisfying than a home that feels safe, friendly, cooperative, and harmonious.

Conclusion

Picture yourself trying to pick up and move a large table to another room. Now picture moving that same table with a person at each side, everyone holding up their end and moving in unison to relocate the piece of furniture. Or how about this picture: You've decided to have a party for thirty. You do the menu planning, the invitations, the shopping, the cooking, the decorating, the serving, and the cleanup yourself. Now picture gathering a group of people, each with a special talent, to work as a team on the same project. Although you could probably accomplish both projects with or without teamwork, working together for a common goal is more powerful and fulfilling.

We know you will gain a sense of achievement and harmony by involving others in family responsibilities. When you honor the talents and abilities of the others, you create a sense of community. There is no finish line once you get involved in this process, but that makes being a family much more fun. Adding and changing is what growth is all about, and growth is what keeps us healthy.

The more you practice the ideas in *Chores Without Wars*, the more you realize that you are working on relationships rather than just tasks. Your relationships will become more satisfying and respectful when everyone experiences belonging and

189

significance through contributing. The fact that you'll also get a lot of help with the chores and that your family members will be more skilled and happier are added bonuses.

Trust the process and have faith when the going gets tough. Your actions influence generations to come, so what you do now is worth the extra effort. Keep the bigger picture in mind as you take each small step, and soon you'll look back and have a hard time remembering when things weren't always this way.

Start now. Take small steps and act. Have courage to vault the hurdles. People who feel capable, needed, and self-reliant lead healthier lives. You can realize your dreams for a more cooperative family by moving toward making yours *Chores Without Wars*.

Beaver . . .
Teach me to build my dreams,
Including others too.
One mind,
One thought,
Hearts as one,
Lessons learned from you.[1]

---

1. *Medicine Cards: The Discovery of Power Through the Ways of Animals,* Jamie Sams and David Carson (Santa Fe, New Mexico: Bear & Company, 1988), p. 124.

Bibliography

Adler, Alfred. *What Life Should Mean To You*. New York: Capricorn Books, 1958.

———. *Superiority and Social Interest*. Illinois: Northwestern University Press, 1964.

———. *Social Interest*. New York: Capricorn Books, 1964.

———. *Cooperation Between the Sexes*. New York: Anchor Books, 1978.

Albert, Linda. *Coping with Kids*. New York: E. P. Dutton, 1982.

Allred, G. Hugh. *How to Strengthen Your Marriage and Family*. Provo, UT: Brigham Young University Press, 1976.

Ansbacher, Heinz and Rowena. *The Individual Psychology of Alfred Adler*. New York: Harper Touchbooks, 1964.

Bayard, Robert and Jean. *How to Deal with Your Acting Up Teenager*. San Jose, CA: The Accord Press, 1981.

Beecher, Marguerite and Willard. *Beyond Success and Failure*. New York: Pocket Books, 1966.

Bettner, Betty Lou and Amy Lew. *Raising Kids Who Can*. New York: Harper Perennial, 1992.

Cassel, Pearl, and Raymond J. Corsini. *Coping with Teenagers in a Democracy*. Toronto: Lugus, 1990.

Christiensen, Oscar. *Adlerian Family Counseling*. Minneapolis, MN: Educational Media Corp., 1983.

Corsini, Raymond, and Genevieve Painter. *The Practical Parent*. New York: Harper and Row, 1975.

Deline, John. *Who's Raising the Family?* Madison, WI: Wisconsin Clearing House, 1981.

Dinkmeyer, Don, and Rudolf Dreikurs. *Encouraging Children to Learn: The Encouragement Process*. Englewood Cliffs, NJ: Prentice-Hall, 1963.

Dinkmeyer, Don, and Gary McKay. *Parents Handbook: Systematic Training for Effective Parenting* (3rd edition). Circle Pines, MN: American Guidance Service, Inc., 1989.

Dinkmeyer, Don, and Gary McKay. *Raising a Responsible Child.* New York: Simon & Schuster, 1973.

Dinkmeyer, Don, W. L. Pew, and Don Dinkmeyer Jr. *Adlerian Counseling and Psychotherapy.* Monterey, CA: Brooks/Cole Publishing, 1979.

Dreikurs, Rudolf. *Social Equality: The Challenge of Today.* Chicago: Contemporary Books, Inc., 1971.

———. *Psychology in the Classroom.* New York: Harper & Row, 1966.

———. Corsini, and S. Gould. *Family Council.* Chicago: Henry Regnery, 1974.

Dreikurs, Rudolf, Bronia Grunwald, and Floyd Pepper. *Maintaining Sanity in the Classroom.* New York: Harper & Row, 1971.

Dreikurs, Rudolf, and V. Soltz. *Children: The Challenge.* New York: Hawthorn Books, 1964.

Dyer, Wayne. *Your Erroneous Zones.* New York: Avon Books, 1976.

Glenn, H. Stephen, and Jane Nelsen. *Raising Self-Reliant Children in a Self-Indulgent World.* Rocklin, CA: Prima Publishing, 1988. (1-800-456-7770).

Glenn, H. Stephen. *Developing Capable People* (audio cassette tape set). Fair Oaks, CA: Sunrise Press. (1-800-456-7770)

———. *Bridging Troubled Waters* (audio cassette tape set). Fair Oaks, CA: Sunrise Press, 1989. (1-800-456-7770).

———. *Involving and Motivating People* (audio cassette tape). Fair Oaks, CA: Sunrise Press. (1-800-456-7770).

———. *Introduction to Developing Capable People* (video tape). Fair Oaks, CA: Sunrise Press, 1989. (1-800-456-7770).

———. *Empowering Others: Ten Keys to Affirming and Validating People* (video tape). Fair Oaks, CA: Sunrise Press, 1989. (1-800-456-7770).

———. *The Greatest Human Need* (video tape). Fair Oaks, CA: Sunrise Press, 1989. (1-800-456-7770).

———. *Six Steps to Developing Responsibility* (video tape). Fair Oaks, CA: Sunrise Press, 1989. (1-800-456-7770).

———. *Developing Healthy Self-Esteem* (video tape). Fair Oaks, CA: Sunrise Press, 1989. (1-800-456-7770).

———. *Teachers Who Make a Difference* (video tape). Fair Oaks, CA: Sunrise Press, 1989. (1-800-4456-7770).

Goldberg, Herb. *Hazards of Being Male.* New York: New American Library, 1976.

Janoe, Ed and Barbara. *Dealing with Feelings.* Vancouver, WA: Arco Press, 1973.

———. *About Anger.* Vancouver, WA: Arco Press, 1973.

Kvols-Reidler, Bill and Kathy. *Redirecting Children's Misbehavior.* Boulder, CO: R.D.I.C. Publications, 1979.

Losoney, Lewis. *You Can Do It.* New Jersey: Prentice-Hall, Inc., 1980.

Lott, Lynn, Marilyn Kentz, and Dru West. *To Know Me Is To Love Me.* Santa Rosa, CA: The Practical Press, 1983. (1-800-456-7770).

Lott, Lynn, and Dru West. *Together and Liking It* (formerly *Married and Liking It).* Santa Rosa, CA: The Practical Press, 1987. (1-800-456-7770).

Lott, Lynn, and Jane Nelsen. *Teaching Parenting Manual.* Fair Oaks, CA: Sunrise Press, 1990.

Manaster, Guy J., and Raymond Corsini. *Individual Psychology.* Itasca, IL: F. E. Peacock Publishers, Inc., 1982.

Nelsen, Jane. *Positive Discipline.* New York: Ballantine Books, 1987. (Originally published in 1981 by Sunrise Press, Fair Oaks, CA.) (1-800-456-7770).

———. *Understanding: Eliminating Stress and Finding Serenity in Life and Relationships.* Rocklin, CA: Prima Publishing, 1988. (Originally published in 1986 by Sunrise Press, Fair Oaks, CA.) (1-800-456-7770).

———. *Positive Discipline* (audio cassette tape). Fair Oaks, CA: Sunrise Press (1-800-456-7770).

———. *Positive Discipline* (video). Fair Oaks, CA: Sunrise Press, 1988. (1-800-456-7770).

———. *Positive Discipline Study Guide.* Fair Oaks, CA: Sunrise Press, 1988. (1-800-456-7770).

Nelsen, Jane, and H. Stephen Glenn. *Time Out: Abuses and Effective Uses.* Fair Oaks, CA: Sunrise Press, 1991. (1-800-456-7770).

Nelsen, Jane, Riki Intner, and Lynn Lott. *Positive Discipline for Parenting in Recovery.* Rocklin, CA: Prima Publishing, 1996. (1-800-456-7770).

Nelsen, Jane, Lynn Lott, and H. Stephen Glenn. *Positive Discipline in the Classroom.* Rocklin, CA: Prima Publishing, 1997. (1-800-456-7770).

———. *Positive Discipline: A–Z.* Rocklin, CA: Prima Publishing, 1993. (1-800-456-7770).

Nelsen, Jane, and Lynn Lott. *Positive Discipline for Teenagers.* (formerly *I'm on Your Side)* Rocklin, CA: Prima Publishing, 1994. (1-800-456-7770).

Nelsen, Jane, Cheryl Erwin, and Carol Delzer. *Positive Discipline for Single Parents.* Rocklin, CA; Prima Publishing, 1994. (1-800-456-7770).

Pew, W. L., and J. Terner. *Courage to Be Imperfect.* New York: Hawthorn Books, 1978.

Smith, Manuel J. *When I Say No I Feel Guilty.* New York: The Dial Press, 1975.

Walton, F.X., *Winning Teenagers Over.* Columbia, SC: Adlerian Child Care Books Publishing, 1994.

Index